Lloyd & MaryNell,

May God bless
you with abundant
prosperity

God's Prosperity Plan

Rod Nichols

Tim Johnson

Copyright © 2004 by Rod Nichols & Tim Johnson

ISBN 0-7414-2106-2

Published by:

PUBLISHING.COM

1094 New Dehaven Street, Suite 100
West Conshohocken, PA 19428-2713
Info@buybooksontheweb.com
www.buybooksontheweb.com
Toll-free (877) BUY BOOK
Local Phone (610) 941-9999
Fax (610) 941-9959

Printed in the United States of America

Printed on Recycled Paper

Published July 2004

Acknowledgements

We dedicate this book first to Jesus who came to earth and died for our sins, so that we might live an abundant life here on earth and an eternal life in heaven. We thank God for His saving grace and for His Word that guides our lives. We thank Him for leading us in the development of God's Prosperity Plan and for the tremendous blessings that have resulted.

We also dedicate this book to Bill and Eva Dorsey, for the financial gift and prayer that made publishing possible. Thank you for your love and support.

Rod: I dedicate this book to my wonderful wife Karen. Thank you for your love, support, and editing. This book is better because of you. I love you and our abundant life together.

Tim: I dedicate this book to my parents, Duane and Eileen Johnson for your faithfulness and wisdom in raising me in the church and in the truth. It was through your Godly example that I learned how to walk by faith, how to apply the principles of sowing and reaping, and how to stand on the Word regardless of external circumstances. Mom and Dad, I shall forever be indebted to you and I love you deeply.

Table of Contents

Introduction

How would you like to have $10,000 mysteriously appear in your bank account? How about if $20,000 worth of your debt just disappeared? What about a job offer working fewer hours and making twice as much? These are just a few of the many miraculous experiences of those who are operating in God's Prosperity Plan. They too were once operating in the world's plan, but after studying the material contained in this book, made a few changes and are now reaping rich benefits in this life and storing up treasures in heaven for their eternal life.

Many people, who attend church regularly, have gotten the impression that money is bad and that it is holy to be poor. Up until now Satan has done a great job of deceiving God's children, but now God wants the truth revealed. This book contains the truth and nothing but the truth, based on the Word of God. Some will choose to believe the truth and begin operating in God's plan. Others will choose to continue living according to the lies of the devil and stick with the world's plan. However, one day all of us will stand before God and give an accounting of our life. Those who ignored God's plan and lived by the world's plan will have a hard time explaining their actions.

What is the world's plan? It's explained quite well on bumper stickers – "He who dies with the most toys wins!" In the eyes of the world, those people with the greatest amount of material wealth are the real winners. The problem with that is that money and material things are only temporary, while spiritual things are eternal. The key here is that we are transcending two realms; the physical and the spiritual. The world's plan operates only in the physical realm (the world we can see). However God's plan operates in both the physical and spiritual (that which we cannot see) realms. God wants us to be prosperous in both realms.

This book contains the principles of God's prosperity plan. It will teach you how to be prosperous both here on earth and in heaven. It was developed after years of prayer and petition. The principles were first taught in a class by the same title, in the spring of 2001. The fruit from the class was amazing, as the students put these simple principles into action in their lives. Spiritual and financial blessings were abundant in all of their lives. You will encounter many of these amazing stories throughout the book.

The world wants you to believe that their way is the best: climbing the corporate ladder, while disregarding your family; get rich quick schemes that require no work and you make millions; the lottery and gambling; zero down real estate investing; and so on. While there is nothing wrong with real estate and investing, it is best if you seek God first, He will open those doors for you.

God wants His children to be the most prosperous people on earth. Unfortunately many Christians have been taught that prosperity is sinful. Scriptures such as Matthew 19:24, "Again I tell you, it is easier for a camel to go through the eye of a needle than for a rich man to enter the kingdom of God", have been used to misinform and paralyze Christians. This is all part of Satan's plan to bind the children of God and slow the growth of the Kingdom. After all, who is going to finance the spreading of the gospel, if Christians don't? Who is going to pay for the Bibles? Who is going to send out the missionaries? Who is going to build the orphanages and feed the poor? The world sure isn't, so it's up to us to discover how to tap into God's prosperity plan.

In the following pages, you will learn the qualifications for Divine prosperity. Yes, God does have requirements; there is no free ride in this plan. You will also learn about God's prosperity mindset and how to adopt that into your own life. You will discover the power of sowing into the Kingdom. These pages will introduce you to the power of partnership with the Creator of the world. You will learn to become a good steward of the things that God gives you. Plus you will learn to seek wisdom, instead of money, and find that the money will chase after you, instead of you chasing after it. Lastly, God's plan is not instantaneous, so you'll learn how to survive until complete prosperity arrives by utilizing some practical methods. Finally, you will develop your own personal financial plan.

This book can be used for individual study or you will find discussion questions at the end of each chapter, which allows you to use the book for a group study. If you aren't already involved in a small group, why not gather together a few friends who are all interested in increased prosperity and read through the book together. You can answer the discussion questions ahead of time and then discuss them each time your group meets. This will give God another avenue to speak into your lives and you can pray for each other, which increases the power of this book.

The most exciting part is that everything in this book is solidly based in God's Word, the Bible. It is all God's truth and promises to His children. If you do what God is teaching, you will prosper in all aspects of your life. So, take your time while reading this book. Underline, highlight, dog-ear pages, put sticky notes in key spots, take notes, and most of all meditate over the words that are contained in this book. God will reveal His specific prosperity plan for you!

One

The Divine Prosperity Plan

Chapter 1

The Divine Prosperity Plan

God has a plan to prosper you. He is very clear in His Word, but unfortunately most Christians aren't even aware that this plan exists or they are so bound up in error that they don't believe God really wants them to prosper. In this chapter, you will learn the basics of God's plan. These will then be expanded in the following chapters.

According to the Federal Reserve Board, 54% of total wealth in the U.S. is held by 2% of the families and the top 10% of families hold 86% of the wealth. Most of these families are not Christians and have obtained their wealth using the world's plan. The people of the world are wiser in the ways of prosperity than Christians are. They have listened to the devil better than Christians have listened to God. Jesus said that the world is wiser in the ways of business than the believers are (Luke 16:8). This must change, so that the world can see the immense benefits of following Jesus.

When Jesus walked the earth, he attracted crowds of people through miraculous signs and wonders. He wants to do that again, with regard to your financial situation. Imagine how your friends and family would respond, if in a short period of time you were completely debt free, financially independent, and spending most of your time doing the work of the Lord? If they saw you stress free and joyous all the time, don't you think they would want to know more? That would open up many opportunities for witnessing to the people in your world. That is what God wants. He wants His children to be the most prosperous on the planet. He did that for David and Solomon and He wants to do the same for you.

Yes, God wants to prosper you, but He's not going to do it until you are ready to receive the fullness of His prosperity. He isn't holding back because He doesn't want to bless you, but rather to protect you. If He dumped His blessings upon you and you weren't ready, the devil could use them to deceive you and send you down a very destructive path. I'm sure you've seen examples of this – the multi-million dollar lottery winner, who a year later is divorced and in bankruptcy court. God loves you and wants you to enjoy His prosperity, not find it to be a burden that tears your life apart. So, there is some preparation that must be done, in order to put you into a receiving mode. In the following pages you will learn the qualifications for receiving God's prosperity into your life. If you accomplish these things, you will place yourself into position to receive the blessings of God.

Satan has spent thousands of years setting financial traps for people. He particularly loves to trap Christians and place them into financial bondage. He has used the spirit of mammon to get people focused on money, instead of on God. Then, as the devil finds people who are fully in his camp, he helps them become reservoirs for his money and he blesses them abundantly. He knows that if he pours it on them, they will go out and purchase mansions, luxury cars, flashy jewelry, alcohol, drugs, and take exotic trips. This, of course, will attract other people who want all the same stuff. For most, Satan uses the lure of credit and high interest to completely bind people financially. Then there are the really unfortunate few, whom he totally destroys through gambling. Satan is the great deceiver and he is actively trying to destroy your life through your finances.

God has a different plan. He wants you to focus your eyes and attention on Him first and then He will show you the way. If you seek God with all your heart and do what He tells you to do, God's blessings will chase you down and the financial blessings will be overflowing. You will be a channel for God's prosperity. It will flow into your life and back out into the world to build His Kingdom. Jesus said, "The thief comes only to steal and kill and destroy, I have come that they may have life and have it abundantly." God's plan includes abundance for all of His children.

Throughout the Bible, God has taught people the principle of sowing and reaping. 2 Corinthians 9:6 says, "Whoever sows sparingly will also reap sparingly, and whoever sows generously will also reap generously." This is where you start to understand that God's prosperity plan is the opposite of the world's prosperity plan. With God's plan, you have to give it away in order to receive, whereas in the world, you are taught to hoard. In the following pages, you will learn the secrets of sowing and reaping. It all starts with what you sow into your heart and ends with what you sow financially into the Kingdom. Your prosperity level is dependent on the quality and quantity of your sowing.

There is a woman who is a member of our church and has really grasped this principle. For many years she attended church and gave money at every offering, but she never truly understood the principles of God's prosperity plan. After listening to a few of our tapes, she committed to a consistent tithing and giving program. Within 24 hours she received a letter indicating that she owned some stock (that her Father had purchased). After careful investigation, she determined that the stock was worth at least $30,000. Soon after, she also received a substantial raise at work. Needless to say, she has continued her tithing and giving program and continues to be abundantly blessed.

The world teaches people to be selfish, whereas the Bible teaches selflessness. In the beginning, Adam and Eve sowed disobedience into their lives and into all generations leading up to the death and resurrection of Jesus Christ. They sowed into the flesh rather than the Kingdom. Are you sowing into

4

the flesh or are you focused on and sowing into God's Kingdom? God can only bless that which is sowed into the Spirit.

God's plan teaches us that our heart is a garden and whatever we sow into that soil, whether good or bad, will grow. If you plant the seeds of God's promises for prosperity, then you will reap an abundant and prosperous harvest. If you plant worldly seeds into your garden – seeds of greed and selfishness, then you will reap a worldly harvest of financial troubles. In the following pages you will learn about the prosperity promises that God has made in the Bible and how to plant them firmly into your garden, so that you can live a prosperous life.

A huge part of God's plan is the Seed System, which is discussed in 1 Corinthians 3:6, "I have planted, Apollos watered, but God gave the increase." Contrary to the world's view, which says work harder and you will become more prosperous, God's plan requires us to do our part and then He causes the increase. The key here is that we must do our part for the system to work. Later in this book, you will learn more about the seed system and the ways that the devil will try to hinder you. You will also learn how to uncover the things that are keeping you from an abundant harvest.

God gives us seed (money) to eat (money to buy food) and seed to plant (tithes and offerings). 2 Corinthians 9:10 says, "Now he who supplies seed to the sower and bread for food, will also supply and increase your store of seed and will enlarge the harvest of your righteousness." The "he" referenced in this scripture is God and all of the seed belongs to Him; He just lets us have some of it for our own use. Unfortunately, most Christians are eating the seed that was meant for planting and so they are not enjoying the harvest that God had intended.

My wife, Karen and I (Rod) were in that situation a number of years ago. Things were tough financially and we were not tithing consistently. We would pay all the bills and if there was enough left over, we would tithe. If we were unable to tithe or it was short, we would promise God to make up the difference later. It wasn't until we really got the principle of tithing and started writing that check first, that the financial blessings were abundant. Since then we have always written the tithe check first and there has always been more than enough money. Our money goes further and now we are able to give above and beyond the tithe.

Further along in this book, you will learn what God's Word says about planting. You will learn the truth about tithes and offerings. Both are independently powerful and critical to God's plan.

In school we learn about multiplication – the world's way. However, God teaches us about multiplication throughout the Bible. He has His own system of multiplication that is much grander than that of the world. You will learn how to plant your seed and see a hundred fold return. What worldly investor wouldn't like to invest $1000 and receive $100,000 in return? The great part about God's multiplication system is that it's up to Him how much He increases; after all He is a Father who loves to bless His kids.

The world teaches us to save for a rainy day; that you get ahead by putting money away. There is some truth to this, but mostly it is truth that has been twisted by the devil, so that it sounds good. The truth is that the world's system doesn't really work. The Word tells us that sowing causes increase and hoarding causes curses (Proverbs 11:24-28). When God gives us seed to plant, He wants us to plant it in good soil (Kingdom soil), not in a worldly bank or other financial vehicle. When you put all your extra money into a bank, you are hoarding and falling into one of Satan's traps. However, when you plant that money into the Kingdom – church, missions, or good ministries, you will receive God's blessings, which are much better than the interest or dividends you might earn with those earthly investments.

6

When God created our world, He established some natural laws like gravity and aerodynamics which rule our natural world activities. He also established spiritual laws that rule the spiritual realm. By understanding these laws, you will have the opportunity to fully tap into God's prosperity plan. One of these is the law of reciprocity – in other words, what goes around, comes around. If you lay up treasures here on earth, your benefit will be only here on earth, whereas if you lay up treasures in heaven, you will reap eternal benefits. Later in this book you will learn more about these laws and how they relate to prosperity in the natural world. Gaining a complete understanding of spiritual laws will help you transcend into natural world activities.

The world is very familiar with partnerships – marriage and business partnerships are the most widely known of the earthly partnerships. God created partnerships and wants to be your partner. The apostle Paul talks about this in Philippians 4:10-20. He has put his trust totally in God and is content with whatever He provides; whether living in plenty or in want. Yet, he is commending the Philippians for partnering with God through him. God anoints certain people, such as Paul, to spread the Gospel, and when we partner with them through our giving, we receive the reward of partnering with God. Paul talks about that reward in verse 19, when he says, "And my God will meet all your needs according to his glorious riches in Christ Jesus." Wouldn't you like to have access to God's glorious riches? After all, He walks on streets of gold and is surrounded by precious stones of all types. God's storehouse of riches is available to those who partner with Him.

In order to be a good partner, we must become good stewards of what God gives us. It is He who has given us the talents and abilities to obtain wealth. Deuteronomy 8:18 says, "But you shall remember the Lord your God, for it is He who gives you power to get wealth . . ." There are only two roads to wealth – Satan's or God's. We cannot achieve wealth on our own. Satan's way is the world's way and it only works in this world and eventually leads to destruction. How many times have you read headlines or watched news stories about highly successful musicians, actors, or business people who take their own life. Satan hates mankind, so his only motivation for blessing people who follow him (either directly or inadvertently by not serving God), is to destroy them through greed and selfishness. God, on the other hand, does want His children to enjoy life here on earth, but also wants to protect them from destruction at the hands of the devil. If you believe God's promises, then He has given you the power to achieve wealth. Proverbs 10:22 says, "The blessing of the Lord brings wealth, and he adds no trouble to it." All you have to do is discover those talents, skills, and abilities, and then put them to work in God's prosperity plan and He will bless you abundantly.

God also provides money to people according to their ability to handle it. He provides a little extra to see how you handle it, much like the Parable of the Talents (Matthew 25:14-30) that Jesus told. If you handle it well, you are rewarded with more. If you mishandle it, quite often even what you have will be taken away. Many Christians are living paycheck to paycheck because they haven't learned to be good stewards of the money God has provided. The devil usually has a big part in this, as he uses credit to tempt Christians into debt, which is not good stewardship. The key aspect of God's plan is to get your eyes and focus off the money and on to God. Then when God provides you with an increase, ask Him how you should use the extra money. He will provide the direction.

Solomon was given the opportunity to have anything he wanted. Instead of asking for wealth, he asked God for His direction, in the form of wisdom. Because of Solomon's faithfulness, God rewarded him with wisdom, wealth, and a long healthy life. You can learn a valuable lesson from God's prosperity plan through Solomon's story – seek wisdom and wealth will follow. As you will learn further into this book, wisdom is obtained through daily reading of

God's Word, through Spirit-filled church services, in classes with Bible-based teaching, and through times of prayer with the Lord. Wisdom is a popular topic in the Bible, which means that it is very important to God and thus should also be very important to us.

There are seven incredible benefits of God's wisdom that will be studied in this book. They are accurate judgment, success, honor, wealth, knowledge, enjoyment, and balance. People spend years seeking these benefits through worldly teachings and activities, yet they are never able to fully achieve them. This is because the world's wisdom is so very weak compared to God's infinite wisdom. So, the choice is yours, you can continue to seek the world's wisdom or tap into the all-knowing wisdom of your heavenly Father.

Although it is the Father's will that His children prosper, He decides when you are ready. Until that time, the bills still need to get paid, the children need to be fed, and you still have to put gas into the car, so you'll need to know what to do until prosperity arrives. First, you need to put your complete trust in the Lord; that He is in control, not the world. Satan will use times like this to put fear into your heart and try to make you doubt that God is really there or that He really cares about your circumstances or that He's too busy running the universe to really care about your small situation. None of this is the truth. The truth is that God cares about every hair on your head and every circumstance in your life. We have seen so many examples of this, but there is one that really stands out. A friend of ours was seeking the Lord with all his heart, reading and meditating on the Word and investing time in prayer every day, attending all the church services, serving at the church, tithing and giving faithfully, serving his family, and working for the Lord at his job. He seemed to be doing everything right, yet the company he was working for went out of business and then a business alliance went awry. He and his family struggled financially for a year. Through it all, he never gave up on God and continued to serve him faithfully.

Today he has been blessed with a very successful business and has purchased a large, new home. As with our friend, God wants to prosper you, but He will do it in His timing, not yours.

Next, you need to plant all of God's prosperity promises firmly in your heart, so that none of that doubt or fear can take root. Then, stand and wait until God moves. Don't do anything unless God tells you to. Remember Jesus said that He did nothing but what He first saw the Father do. So, spend time in prayer and meditation over the Word every day, so that you can always know the will of God for your life that day. Also, no complaining! When you complain, you show God that you doubt Him. If you are going to make God Lord of your life, then you have to give Him all of it. In Philippians 4:10-13 we see that the apostle Paul had learned how to be content with whatever God gave him and you need to learn to do the same. Believe that God will bring you prosperity, do the things that He shows you to do, and prosperity will come.

Following that you will learn some practical keys for prosperity taught in the Bible. You will learn about the power of tithing and giving. God is very clear about the importance of the tithe; the blessings that you will receive if you tithe and the curses that will overtake you if you don't. Many people believe that the tithe isn't necessary any more; that it was abolished when Jesus brought the new covenant into the world. However, this is not true and you will learn what Jesus had to say about the tithe. Giving is another powerful part of God's prosperity plan – maybe the most important. We will show you how and where to give, so that all of your seed is planted in good soil, watered, and ready for God's increase. A couple who attended our God's Prosperity Plan class had been in church for many years, but hadn't been tithing, because they thought it wasn't a New Testament principle. They took the teaching on the tithe very seriously and within a few months were blessed with a significant raise and a large sum of money that they didn't know was owed to them.

After you have learned all the lessons the Bible has to teach, you will learn how to apply them to your current financial situation. An area that has huge impact on most people is credit. God is against it! Unfortunately the financial world has been built around it. If you have even halfway decent credit, you likely get five to ten solicitations for credit cards or loans every week. Near the end of this book, you will learn how to quickly reduce your credit card debt, payoff your mortgage and auto loans quicker, and terminate debt all together. God wants you to live a debt-free life. When you put your trust in banks and credit card companies, you are not showing faith in God. You will also discover how to budget effectively and how God will provide you with opportunities to develop additional income sources. God's plan calls for us to live on 10% of what we make (and yet live very comfortably) and give away 90% to benefit the Kingdom. You will learn how to accomplish this goal within your lifetime.

God wants you to be prosperous. He has a divine prosperity plan for your life. Your choice is to either stay in the world and struggle or tap into God's prosperity plan and live a joyous and prosperous life. If you choose God's plan, then continue on to the next chapter. If you choose to continue in the world's ways, then you might as well close this book right now and give it to someone who might like to enjoy God's prosperity in their life and is willing to meet the qualifications for His plan.

1. Should Christians be prosperous? Support your reasons with scripture if possible.

2. If Satan hates mankind, why would he want to help people prosper?

3. What would the world be like if all Christians were living prosperous lives?

4. What are some of the financial traps that Satan sets for people?

5. Why does God limit the amount of money a person receives?

6. Read Philippians 4:10-13 and discuss how Paul could have learned to be content.

7. Are you ready to embark on this adventure? If so, why?

Two

Qualifications for Divine Prosperity

Chapter 2

Qualifications for Divine Prosperity

God wants all of His children to be prosperous in all aspects of their life; however He also lists some qualifications in His Word. It's not that He wants to make it difficult; it's that He wants us to be properly prepared to receive and handle prosperity. Otherwise, if we were not prepared, we could get caught up in the world and turn away from God. In the following pages, you will learn about the qualifications and how you can meet them.

Qualification One: Born-Again Believer

John 3:3 says, "I tell you the truth, no one can see the Kingdom of God unless he is born again." Would God's prosperity be part of the Kingdom of God? Well, let's examine that. One definition of the Kingdom of God is "Christ's mediatorial authority or His rule here on earth and the blessings and advantages of all kinds that flow from his rule." Is prosperity a blessing from God? Must you be born-again in order to receive that blessing? If we fully believe in the scriptures, then it is so.

Now, you might be wondering about all the wealthy people who aren't born-again. Satan blesses people also. People are either in God's camp or Satan's camp. There is no in between ground. If a person is not following Jesus, then they are following Satan. It may not be a conscious choice, but rather an unconscious choice. They are choosing the ways of the world and those are the devil's ways.

Proverbs 13:22 says that a sinner's wealth is stored up for the righteous. How did that sinner get wealthy? It sure wasn't God's blessings, so it must have been Satan. The devil is looking for people to become reservoirs; people who will hoard the money he blesses them with and keep it out of the hands of the righteous. God, on the other hand, is looking for channels; people who will channel His financial blessings into Kingdom work.

You can be blessed either through the world's prosperity plan or God's plan. The choice is yours. If you are born-again, then you instantly meet the first qualification for God's prosperity plan. If you are not born-again or don't even know what that means, you can refer to John 3:5, where Jesus said, "I tell you the truth, no one can enter the kingdom of God unless he is born of water and the Spirit." What this means is that you must accept the living water of Jesus Christ into your life and make Him Lord of your entire life. By doing this you will receive the Holy Spirit, who will dwell within your spirit to guide you the rest of your life. Ask God for forgiveness of your sins and then ask Jesus to come into your heart and become Lord of your life. If you truly are repentant and mean it, you will be born again. Romans 10:9-10 says, "That if you confess with your mouth, 'Jesus is Lord,' and believe in your heart that God raised him from the dead, you will be saved. For it is with your heart that you believe and are justified, and it is with your mouth that you confess and are saved." Make sure you get connected with a good church, so that the Pastors can guide you through the next steps.

Qualification Two: Favor God's Righteous Cause

It is one thing to be born-again and then go on with life. It is quite another to be born-again and favor God's righteous cause. Psalm 35:27 says, "Let them shout for joy and be glad, who favor my righteous cause; And let them say continually, 'let the Lord be magnified, who has pleasure in the prosperity of His servant.'" What is God's righteous cause? Jesus answered that question when he gave the disciples the "great commission." In Matthew 28:18-20, Jesus said, "All authority has been given to Me in heaven

15

and on earth. Go therefore and make disciples of all the nations, baptizing them in the name of the Father and of the Son and of the Holy Spirit, teaching them to observe all things that I have commanded you. . ."

The apostle Paul understood about God's righteous cause, as you can see in Acts 16:10, where it says, "After Paul had seen the vision, we got ready at once to leave for Macedonia, concluding that God had called us to preach the gospel to them." God's righteous cause is spreading the gospel to everyone in the world. In Paul's case, he was called to literally preach the gospel. Pastors and Evangelists have the same calling. You may or may not have that calling on your life. If you don't know, seek God for His will. If you do have a calling to preach, then get out and preach the gospel wherever you can – it doesn't have to be in church. If you are not called to preach, you can still spread the good Word of Jesus Christ through your testimony, funding for your local church and other good ministries, and by speaking to friends and family about Jesus.

God has called all of us to have a part in His righteous cause. According to Matthew 5:16, Matthew 13:43 and Philippians 2:15, we are to shine the light of Jesus on people through our words and actions. A friend of ours was out playing golf one day with a couple guys he didn't know. After the first nine holes, one of the guys asked if he was a pastor. He was surprised at the question, as they had not talked about occupation at all. He answered, "Yes" and the man who asked the question said that he figured as much, because no normal person could play as badly as he had without swearing at least once. Are you allowing Jesus to shine through your actions? Can people tell you are a follower of Christ by the way you live your life?

Another way that we can favor God's righteous cause is through tithing and giving. All Believers are called to tithe faithfully. Deuteronomy 14:22 and Proverbs 3:9-10 tell us to tithe, which means to give the first 10% of everything God gives us. Malachi 3:10, tells us that we should be tithing to the local storehouse. In Old Testament times, the temple had a storehouse, so that people could bring in the first fruits of their labor – grain, fruit, vegetables, and livestock. Today, the storehouse is the church where God has placed you and is feeding you. Leviticus 27:30 shows us that the tithe is Holy, which means that it belongs to God. If you are spending what you should be tithing, then you are messing with something Holy. Malachi 3:8 teaches us that if we are not giving the tithe to God, we are stealing from Him and will be cursed. However verses 10 and 11 tell us that if we do tithe that we will be blessed in a couple of ways (discussed later in the book). Tithing is not something from the Old Testament law that was abolished by the new covenant of Jesus; it is still a major part of God's prosperity plan. One attendee of our God's Prosperity Plan class had been in the church for over 20 years, but had never fully understood the tithe. Through the class he gained crystal clear understanding and began tithing 10% of his gross income. Within a few weeks he received an unexpected raise and a substantial bonus, with another surprise bonus check arriving several weeks later.

God also calls us to be generous and cheerful givers, above the tithe. When we go to a restaurant, we don't hesitate to tip the waiter or waitress 15% or better, so why should God receive just 10%? Deuteronomy 15:10 says, "Give generously to him and do so without a grudging heart; then because of this the Lord your God will bless you in all your work and in everything you put your hand to." Proverbs 11:25 says that a generous man will prosper. Proverbs 22:9 says that a generous man will be blessed. In 1st Timothy 6:18, Paul instructs, "Command them to do good, to be rich in good deeds, and to be generous and willing to share." Everything we have belongs to God and He wants us to be generous with it. Tithing is commanded; it's something we must do in obedience to God. However, giving is our opportunity to show God how much we love

Him. So, give generously and cheerfully, for as it says in 2 Corinthians 9:7, God loves a cheerful giver!

A great way to do this is to set a giving percentage and then increase it by a percentage or dollar amount every month. This will force you to stretch your faith muscles and rely more on God as your source. I (Tim) have done this throughout my life and have seen tremendous benefits. God has always met all my needs, plus he has blessed me abundantly on numerous occasions. He has blessed me with a beautiful, loving wife, a precious daughter, a beautiful house on the water, and a new, luxury SUV. God loves to give back to His kids who are cheerful givers, because He knows that when He blesses a cheerful giver, they will give even more and it is that giving that finances the growth of God's Kingdom on earth.

In order to tap into God's prosperity plan, we must favor God's righteous cause; which is spreading the gospel throughout the world. We each have a part to play, so find your part and begin to fulfill your calling.

Qualification Three: Love God, Not Money

God wants all of His kids to prosper, but not at the expense of losing their love. Money and the things that money can buy can easily become idols. Jesus warned of this in Luke 16:13, "No one can serve both God and money." We need to focus our love on God, not on money or the material things of the world. Our love for God is eternal and has everlasting benefits, whereas the things of this world will one day pass away. Plus, money and material stuff cannot possibly satisfy our hunger; that can only be filled by God. Ecclesiastes 5:10 says, "Whoever loves money never has money enough; whoever loves wealth is never satisfied with his income." You have probably witnessed this either in your own life or the lives of others. They think that the next promotion or the better job or the next big business will satisfy their hunger, only to get there and want more. At this point, more money is the goal and not a loving relationship with God. In Matthew 19:16, we read about a rich young man who approaches Jesus and asks what he needs to do to secure eternal life. Jesus tells him he must obey all the commandments and should sell everything he has, give it to the poor, and follow Him. The rich young man was saddened because he had great wealth and did not want to give it up. When someone puts money before God, he cannot possibly be blessed by God.

When you make God the Lord of your life; your finances must be included. So many Christians tell God that He can be Lord of everything, but their finances. If God is truly Lord, then He is your source; not your job, business, investment portfolio, real estate investments, or the government. However, if you are not fully in obedience in this area, you are not yet qualified to receive His prosperity. If you haven't given up your finances to God and you were to get blessed with prosperity, it would quickly destroy your life. He loves you way too much to let that happen, so He will keep you at a financial level according to your level of financial obedience.

Before you get too far into this book, you need to check your motives. Are you seeking prosperity or are you seeking God. In Luke 10:27, Jesus told us that the most important commandment is to love the Lord with all our heart, soul, mind, and strength. So, in order to qualify for God's prosperity plan, you must first love the Lord with all your heart, soul, mind, and strength.

Money, in itself is not bad or evil, so just because you like money, doesn't mean that you have a wrong motive. Money is necessary in our society, in order to survive. We must have money for housing, food, clothing, vehicles, and so on. God honors this by providing the skills and talents necessary for us to earn a living. Where the motive gets out of line is when people are seeking wealth, instead of God. The apostle Paul said, "People who want to get rich fall into temptation and a trap and into many foolish and harmful desires that plunge men (and women) into ruin and destruction." (1st Timothy 6:9) Continuing on in verse 10, he teaches that the love of money is the root of all evil. It's not money that is evil; it's the love of money. What's in your heart – do you have a root of greed growing? Are you seeking wealth or God for fulfillment?

One of the true qualifiers for divine prosperity is the condition of your heart. Matthew 6:33 says it best, "Seek first his kingdom and his righteousness, and all these things will be given to you as well." We have seen so many of our students get their eyes off the world and on to God; which has resulted quite often in supernatural financial blessings. When you get your eyes on God and off the money, the money will hunt you down and over take you.

Qualification Four: Believe God Wants You to Prosper

It's so unfortunate that on the whole, the Christian community is living in poverty. The worldly people are much wiser when it comes to finances than God's people. Why has this happened? It's been a plan of the devil since the very beginning, to keep God's people in financial bondage. He has done this by twisting the truth – "money is the root of all evil;" "rich people can't get into heaven," and so on. There is some biblical truth at the basis of these statements; however they are not true statements. The devil wants you to believe that it's bad to be rich and that it is holy to be poor. That is a lie from the father of lies himself. Poverty is a curse from the devil that no Believer should accept. The good news is that according to Galatians 3:13, Jesus redeemed us from ALL curses (including poverty). His very first sermon revealed this, "The Spirit of the Lord is on me, because he has anointed me to preach good news to the poor." (Luke 4:18) Part of His mission was to teach the poor that they didn't have to be poor – in spirit or financially!

Do you truly believe that God wants you to prosper? Do you believe that the scriptures are really God's inspired words? If so, then read the following scriptures:

Psalm 35:27 – "Let them shout for joy and be glad, who favor my righteous cause; and let them say continually, 'Let the Lord be magnified, Who has pleasure in the prosperity of His servant.'"

Psalm 112:3 – "Wealth and riches will be in his house, and his righteousness endures forever."

Proverbs 10:22 – "The blessing of the Lord makes one rich, and He adds no sorrow with it."

Psalm 1:1-3 – "Blessed is the man who walks not in the counsel of the ungodly, nor stands in the path of sinners, nor sits in the seat of the scornful; But his delight is the law of the Lord, and in his law he meditates day and night. He shall be like a tree planted by the rivers of water, that brings forth its fruit in its season; whose leaf also shall not wither, and whatever he does shall prosper."

Joshua 1:8 - "This Book of the Law shall not depart from your mouth, but you shall meditate on it day and night, that you may observe to do according to all that is written in it. For then you will make your way prosperous and then you will have good success."

2 Corinthians 9:11 - "You will be made rich in every way so that you can be generous on every occasion and through us your generosity will result in thanksgiving to God."

Isaiah 48:15 – "I, even I, have spoken; Yes, I called him, I have brought him, and his way will prosper."

Isaiah 52:13 – "Behold, My servant will prosper, He will be high and lifted up and greatly exalted." (These are prophetic words about Jesus, who gave us everything the Father gave to Him)

Jeremiah 29:11 – "For I know the plans I have for you," declares the Lord, "plans to prosper you and not to harm you, plans to give you hope and a future."

2 Chronicles 26:5 – "He sought God in the days of Zechariah, who had understanding in visions of God, and as long as he sought the Lord, God made him prosper."

Deuteronomy 29:9 - "Therefore keep the words of this covenant, and do them, that you may prosper in all that you do."

Deuteronomy 30:9 – "Then the Lord your God will make you most prosperous in all the work of your hands, and in the fruit of your womb of your livestock, and the crops of your land. The Lord will again delight in you and make you prosperous, just as he delighted in your fathers."

Proverbs 13:21 – "Misfortune pursues the sinner, but prosperity is the reward of the righteous."

Proverbs 28:25 – "A greedy man stirs up dissension, but he who trusts in the Lord will prosper."

Luke 16:9 – "I tell you, use worldly wealth to gain friends for yourselves, so that when it is gone, you will be welcomed into eternal dwellings."

3 John1:2 – "Beloved, I pray that you may prosper in all things and be in health, just as your soul prospers."

If you truly believe that the Bible is the inspired Word of God, how could you not believe that God wants you to prosper? In fact, God wants you to have so much money that it flows out on people in need and into Kingdom work. However, you have to first believe, before you can receive. If the blessings sound good to you, then strive to meet this qualification for God's prosperity plan.

Qualification Five: Patience Is Truly a Virtue

Lord, give me patience and I want it right now! Isn't that how you feel at those times when God's timing is different than yours? God wants you to be prosperous, but He's going to give it to you in His time, not yours. Since we must wait for God's blessing of prosperity, we will need patience. In Galatians 5 starting in verse 16, Paul talks about walking in the Spirit. In verse 22 he lists the fruit of the Spirit, which includes patience. Those who are walking in the Spirit will have the patience necessary to wait on God.

Romans 15:5 tells us that part of God's character is patience, as it reads, "Now may the God of patience . . ." Since we are made in God's own image, patience is actually part of our character as well. However, the only way we can tap into that part of our character is to get out of the world and get into the Spirit. If you really want to enjoy the benefits of God's plan, then you will need to schedule quiet time with God every day. Learn to just sit and wait on Him. God loves it when we are quiet and wait on Him; that's when He will reward you with knowledge, wisdom, insight, and patience.

James (Jesus' brother) tells us to be patient and stand firm, because the Lord's coming is near (James 5:8). Our human tendency is to be so busy that we don't notice that the Lord is near. Imagine that, the creator of the universe is nearby and wants to prosper us, but we are so busy we don't notice. The much better plan is seek God first, then wait on His instructions before starting.

Another common human error is pride. Sometimes God blesses us and we take credit. It is impossible for proud people to tap into the divine prosperity plan, because they are relying on themselves rather than God.

I (Rod) had many years where I would make up my own business plans and ask God to bless them. I was so prideful that I thought my plans were God's plans, but I learned quickly this was not true as we had to endure financial struggle after financial struggle. Today I've learned to seek God for His plan first and then do what He tells me to do. We now enjoy financial abundance! The Bible says that patience (waiting on God) is better than pride (Ecclesiastes 7:8). If we set aside our pride, we can prove that He is Lord of our life through patience (2 Corinthians 6:6).

Patience is one of the differences between the people of the world and God's holy chosen ones. As God's holy people, we must be clothed in patience, so that the people of the world will see the difference and be attracted to God's plan, rather than the world's plan.

Jesus was our perfect example of patience. 1st Timothy 1:16 says, "But for that very reason I was shown mercy so that in me, the worst of sinners, Christ Jesus might display his unlimited patience as an example for those who would believe on him and receive eternal life." Jesus waited 30 years to begin His ministry. He waited on the Father's timing. He listened and learned from the Father and when it was His time, Jesus began His ministry on earth. God has a prosperous plan for your life. It's your choice, as to whether you race forward on your own or wait patiently for your all knowing, all powerful Heavenly Father to uncover His plan for your life.

Proverbs 19:11 says that a man's wisdom gives him patience. So, how do we obtain wisdom? James 1:5 says that if we lack wisdom, we should ask God, because God gives generously to all without finding fault. However, James continues with a qualification by saying that if a man asks, he must believe and not doubt. God is looking for true believers, not double-minded people. Here we can use Solomon as our example. When God came to Solomon (2 Chronicles) and offered him anything he wanted, Solomon chose wisdom. Because of this God also prospered him greatly.

The last instructions that Jesus gave to His disciples was to wait. In Luke 24:49, Jesus says, "Behold, I send the Promise of My Father upon you; but tarry (wait) in the city of Jerusalem until you are endued (covered) with power from on high (the Holy Spirit)." I (Tim) was 40 when I finally got married. I spent many years waiting on God; asking Him to bring me a wife. At times I was frustrated, but I never doubted God. Today, I have an incredible wife and a wonderful marriage, because I was patient.

Jesus told His followers to be patient and wait on God. As we see in Acts 1, they did wait and did receive the power of the Holy Spirit, which is what enabled them to rapidly build the early church. If they had not been patient, they would have had to build the church on their own power. Just as if we don't wait on God, we have to try to handle finances totally on our own.

We must constantly keep in mind that this is God's plan, not ours. This means that it is also His timing, not ours. This will likely be your biggest challenge – to not charge forward with your own plans, but rather to wait patiently on the Lord for His plan.

Qualification Six: Good Stewardship

God's prosperity plan is progressive. As we meet each qualification, God rewards us with more of His plan. Stewardship is a critical qualification. In biblical times a steward was someone who was hired to take care of the property of another. The closest example we have today would be a property manager. If you owned a large apartment complex and didn't want to manage it yourself, you would hire a property manager. Although the manager does not own the property, you would expect him or her to treat it that way.

We are God's property managers. He has entrusted us with all of his stuff and although we don't own any of it, we are expected to treat it as if we do. All of the money in the world belongs to God. Oh, Satan thinks and acts like it is his and God allows the devil to prosper some people, but actually it all belongs to God and He could take it all back any time He wanted. God entrusts each of us with some of His money. How we handle it, as a steward, will dictate how much we get.

Jesus tells the parable of the talents in Matthew 25:14-30: "Again, it will be like a man going on a journey, who called his servants and entrusted his property to them. To one he gave five talents of money (a talent was worth more than $1000), to another two talents, and to another one talent, each according to his ability." Here we see that the master was entrusting his property to the stewards according to their ability. He did not give any of them more or less than he knew they could handle. God does the same for us. He gives us just as much money as he knows we can handle.

As the parable continues, "Then he (the master) went on his journey. The man who had received the five talents went at once and put his money to work and gained five more. So also, the one with the two talents gained two more." God wants us to take what He gives us and use it wisely, so that it will grow. As you will learn later in the book, the money that God gives us is seed. We are to sow some of it back into the Kingdom and use the rest for our life. The better we get at sowing in both the physical and spiritual realms, the greater the blessings that God will bestow on us.

Jesus continues by saying, "But the man who had received the one talent went off, dug a hole in the ground and hid his master's money. After a long time the master of those servants returned and settled accounts with them. The man who had received the five talents brought the five he had gained with the original five. 'Master,' he said, 'you entrusted me with five talents; see, I have gained five more.' His master replied, 'Well done, good and faithful servant! You have been faithful with a few things; I will put you in charge of many things. Come and share your master's happiness. The man with two talents also came. 'Master,' he said, 'you entrusted me with two talents; see, I have gained two more.' His master replied, 'Well done, good and faithful servant! You have been faithful with a few things; I will put you in charge of many things. Come and share your master's happiness! Then the man who had received the one talent came. 'Master,' he said, 'I knew that you are a hard man, harvesting where you have not sown and gathering where you have not scattered seed. So, I was afraid and went out and hid your talent in the ground. See, here is what belongs to you.' His master replied, 'You wicked, lazy servant! So you knew that I harvest where I have not sown and gather where I have not scattered seed? Well then you should have put my money on deposit with the bankers, so that when I returned I would have received it back with interest. Take the talent from him and give it to the one who has the ten talents. For everyone who has will be given more, and he will have an abundance. Whoever does not have, even what he has will be taken from him. And throw that worthless servant outside, into the darkness, where there will be weeping and gnashing of teeth."

We can learn several lessons from this parable. First, we must always remember that God owns all of the money we have; He is the Master. We are just stewards of the money and anything that it buys. We must always be mindful that God has entrusted us with His money and He, like the master in the parable, expects us to be good stewards of His property. Second, God expects us to grow what He gives us. God expects us to invest all that He gives us wisely – into Kingdom investments (ministries) first and then into solid earthly investments that will produce increase. Third, God will be angry with us if we misuse or don't use what He gives us. If we are selfish and try to do it our way, we will one day stand face to face with the creator and have to give an account of how we used what He gave us. Don't you want to give your account and hear, "Well done, good and faithful servant?" Fourth, if we are faithful with what God gives us, He will reward us with more. So, the key here is to learn to be a good steward, so that God can pour out on your life, abundant prosperity.

To learn more about stewardship, go to Luke 16, the parable of the shrewd manager. This is a very strange parable, because it appears that Jesus is rewarding unscrupulous behavior. Rather, what He is teaching us is how to handle money. The way we handle money is an excellent test of whether Jesus or money is lord of our life. Money, in itself, is neither good nor evil, but it can be used for either. Money, in itself, is not powerful, but it can be used to gain power and manipulate people. Money can rule your life or you can let Jesus rule your money. The choice is yours.

In this parable (Luke 16:10), Jesus reinforces one of the lessons learned in the parable of the talents. He says, "Whoever can be trusted with very little can also be trusted with much, and whoever is dishonest with very little will also be dishonest with much. So, if you have not been trustworthy in handling worldly wealth, who will trust you with true riches?" Money is just a means to a way. It can be used only to gain worldly wealth or it can be used to gain eternal wealth. In Luke 16:9 Jesus says, "I tell you, use worldly wealth to gain friends for yourselves, so that when it is gone, you will be welcomed into eternal dwellings." He is teaching us to use our money to win souls for the Kingdom, as all the worldly things will some day pass away, but we will spend all eternity with the friends we gain. So, in order to be a good steward, you must learn to use the money God gives you to benefit His Kingdom, not just your own.

The great industrialist, R. G. LeTourneau understood this concept, as it is reported he turned over 90% of the assets of his company to a Christian foundation and then he gave away 90% of the income he receive from the remaining 10% ownership. He was reported to have said, "The question is not how much of my money I give to God, but rather how much of God's money I keep." (Page 89, <u>Your Spiritual Gifts</u>, C. Peter Wagner)

One other key to good stewardship is to use only what God gives you. Do not rely on credit to purchase the things of the world. When you use credit, you are putting your trust in a financial institution, rather than in God. When we do use credit, we are operating in the world's plan and God cannot bless it. Proverbs 28:25 says, ". . . but he who trusts in the Lord will prosper." Put your trust in God, not in the world.

Qualification Seven: Love People and Use Money

In the world's prosperity plan people love money and use people. Greed is the name of the game and it is pure evil. Jesus often spoke of the greedy Pharisees. Their focus was on money, material possessions, power, and stature. Because they loved money and used people, they totally missed the Messiah they were waiting for. You too will miss out on the blessings of Jesus, if your focus is on money and what money can buy.

In John 15:12, Jesus said, "My command is this: Love each other as I have loved you." Jesus was not concerned about money or the material things of the world. His mission was to win souls for the Kingdom and break the bondage of sin. His trust was totally in the Father and He loved people unconditionally. In fact, the Father showed His perfect love by sending His only Son, Jesus to die for our sins. Jesus mirrored this perfect love by laying His life down for each of us.

Some day God may allow a situation where you have to lay down your life for someone else. Most people will never be faced with that situation, however, every day you will be faced with the choice of who to make Lord of your finances. Will money be Lord or will God be Lord. As we mentioned earlier, in Matthew 19, Jesus speaks to a rich young man. The young man asks Jesus what he must do to get eternal life. Jesus replies that he must sell his possessions, give the proceeds to the poor, and follow Him. The young man was sad, because he had great wealth. Money was lord of this man's life. Jesus was testing him to see who would truly be lord of his life and he failed. Jesus was not saying that money is bad and that we aren't supposed to have any or that we are supposed to give it all away and be poor. Rather, He was saying that following Him is of greater importance than worldly wealth. The key here is to love Jesus more than you do money.

Psalm 37:3 says, "Trust in the Lord and do good. Then you will live safely in the land and prosper." The Hebrew word for "good" also translates "kind." So this passage could also say, trust in the Lord and be kind. Then you will live safely in the land and prosper. Every day seek out ways to be kind to people. Find ways to show God's love, through you, to others, particularly those who don't know Him. This pleases the Father and He will in turn bless you.

The key to this qualification is the condition of your heart. Is your heart after God or is it after the wealth of the world? God is searching the hearts of His people to find those who have hearts after Him. He passes by those who have hearts after material wealth. So, now is a good time to do a heart check and make sure that you have a heart after the Lord.

Qualification Eight: Be a Generous and Cheerful Giver

Our God is a generous God. Look at all that He gave us? In Genesis it says, "Then God said, 'Let us make man in our image, in our likeness, and let them rule over the fish of the sea and the birds of the air, over the livestock, over all the earth, and over all the creatures that move along the ground.'" (Genesis 1:26) Later, in verse 29 it continues, "Then God said, 'I give you every seed-bearing plant on the face of the whole earth and every tree that has fruit with seed in it. They will be yours for food." In the beginning, God gave us dominion over everything. He made us stewards of the whole world. Unfortunately, as mankind tends to do, we botched it when Adam and Eve sinned by eating of the tree of knowledge and lost dominion to Satan. Fortunately for us, once again, God showed His generosity by sending His only begotten Son to legally regain earthly dominion for mankind.

Our God is a very generous God and since we were made in God's likeness (Genesis 1:26), generosity is also a natural part of our spiritual being. The difficulty is that greed and selfishness are a natural part of our sinful flesh. These two are constantly at odds in our financial decisions. This is why it is important that we walk in the Spirit, when making all financial decisions.

God has many promises for generosity. Psalm 112:5 says, "Good will come to him who is generous. . ." Proverbs 11:25 says, "The generous man will be prosperous and he who waters will himself be watered." Deuteronomy 15:10 says, "Give generously to Him and do so without a grudging heart, then because of this the Lord your God will bless you in all your work and in everything you put your hand to." Proverbs 22:9 says, "A generous man will himself be blessed." In Acts 2 (verse 45) we see generosity and God's promise in action – they sold everything and gave it all away, yet no one was ever in need. 2 Corinthians 9:6 says, "Whoever sows generously will reap generously." 2 Corinthians 9:11 shows us that our generosity will result in riches which enables us to be generous whenever called upon and that becomes a blessing to God.

Imagine being able to give generously whenever something comes along. Think of the people in need you have met and could have blessed. How about your church; there have likely been projects or programs that lacked funds. Karen and I (Rod) were up in Nanimo, BC (Canada) as guest speakers at a Saturday business conference. On Sunday morning we left our hotel room early to find a church. God blessed us with a church service right there in the hotel. It was a small start-up church that was trying to buy a building. They needed $30,000 to complete the funding and there were only about 50 people at the service, so it was going to take some time. We talked about how great it would have been to write a $30,000 check and put it in the offering. Unfortunately, we were not walking in God's plan and so we did not have the funds to be that generous. We did however write a sizeable check that I'm sure helped. God doesn't want us to have to pass up on those opportunities, so we must learn to walk fully in His plan.

When we started our church in January of 2001, we had a group of twelve people and no money. However, those twelve and others God led to the church were all generous givers. Soon we had a place to meet, chairs, tables, computers, office equipment, a sound system, instruments, microwave, refrigerator, and more, all given to us by generous givers. This spirit of generosity continues today as we average tithes and gifts of over $70 a week per person who attends the church. At the writing of this book (April 2003), God just blessed our small church with a 23,000 square foot building for only $5,000 a month and in just six weeks our congregation of about 100 adults raised nearly $23,000 for remodeling.

God not only wants us to be generous givers, but also cheerful givers (2 Corinthians 9:7). There are many Christians who give generously, but they do it out of duty or obligation. This does not bless God. We have to remember that it's not about the money. God walks on streets of gold – He doesn't need the money. It's all about our heart. He wants us to have the Joy of the Lord in our heart that pours out through our giving.

Qualification Nine: We Must Ask

The last of the qualifications for God's plan is that we must ask. When He created us, God gave us free will. He is a Gentleman and will never force anything on you. You could be meeting all the other qualifications and still not be tapped into His plan, because you haven't asked. Matthew 7:7 says that if we ask, it will be given to us. Matthew 7:11 teaches us that God is better than an earthly father who loves to give good gifts to his children. That God will give good gifts to those who ask Him. Matthew 21:22 says, "If you believe, you will receive whatever you ask for in prayer." John 11:22 says, "But I know that even now God will give you whatever you ask." John 14:13 says, "And I will do whatever you ask in my name, so that the Son may bring glory to the Father." John 14:14 says, "You may ask me for anything in my name and I will do it." John 15:7 says, "If you remain in me and my words remain in you, ask whatever you wish, and it will be given to you." John 15:16 says, ". . . Then the Father will give you whatever you ask in my name." John 16:23 says, ". . . I tell you the truth, my Father will give you whatever you ask in my name." It is very clear that we are to ask and ask in the name of Jesus.

God's prosperity plan is available to everyone who would like to partake. However, there are qualifications that need to be met. Now that you have had a chance to review these qualifications, you will need to rate yourself in each area. Are you meeting these qualifications satisfactorily? If so, continue to strive to improve. If not, then it's time to dig into God's Word and begin applying it to your life. Before you can move forward in God's prosperity plan, you must meet all of the qualifications. Here is a quick review of them: (1) Born-again believer; (2) Favor God's righteous cause; (3) Love God, not money; (4) Believe that God wants you to be prosperous; (5) Be patient; (6) Be a good steward; (7) Love people, not money; (8) Be a generous and cheerful giver; (9) Ask. Review God's Prosperity Application on the next page and check off those qualifications you are meeting and those you are not. Complete this step before you move on to the next chapter.

God's Prosperity Application

God doesn't show any favoritism among His children, however He does have some qualifiers that determine who is ready for His divine prosperity and who isn't. In the last chapter you learned about each of these qualifications. Now, it's time to rate yourself and see if you are ready to move on to the next chapter or if you need to spend more time with God in one area or another.

QUESTION	YES	NO
Are you a born-again believer?		
Do you favor God's righteous cause?		
Do you love God, not money?		
Do you believe that God wants you to prosper?		
Are you patient with God's timing?		
Are you a good steward of God's money?		
Do you love people and use money?		
Are you a generous and cheerful giver?		
Are you asking God for prosperity?		

Well, how did you do? If you answered YES to all the questions, then you are ready to move on to Chapter Three: Developing a Prosperity Mindset. If you answered NO to any of the questions, then go back and review that section to determine what you must do in order to meet that qualification. Once you can answer YES to every question, then move on to the next chapter.

Chapter Two Discussion Questions

1. What does it mean to be a "born again believer"?

2. Why must we be "born again" in order to tap into God's prosperity plan?

3. What is God's righteous cause and why is it important to God's plan?

4. Why can't a person serve both God and money?

5. Discuss situations that show a person has not made God Lord of their finances.

6. Do you really believe that God wants you to be wealthy? Discuss your answers.

7. In God's prosperity plan, what does it mean to be patient? Why is this important?

8. What does it mean to be a steward of God's money?

9. Discuss ways in which you have been a good steward of God's money? A bad steward?

10. Why is it important to love people and use money?

11. Are you truly a cheerful giver? Discuss.

12. Discuss some ways that you could be more generous.

13. Why is asking important to entering God's prosperity plan? Discuss.

14. Discuss how you rated yourself on the Application.

Three

Developing a
Prosperity Mindset

Chapter 3

Developing a Prosperity Mindset

God has a prosperity mindset. He knows nothing less than prosperity. Our mission (Mission Impossible theme playing), should we choose to accept it, is to learn how to enter into God's prosperity mindset. The biggest struggle will be that the devil has convinced the world that there are limitations on everything; that there is only one pie and not enough pieces for everyone, so some will have to do without. Satan uses a number of demonic spirits to inhibit our prosperity. So, our first step is to understand how the enemy works to keep us from developing a prosperity mindset.

The enemy is using his demonic duo to stop Christians from receiving the prosperity God intends for them. These two evil spirits are the spirit of religion and the spirit of mammon. He has used these two spirits to keep God's people bound for thousands of years. It's time that we understand and break these bonds, so that God's prosperity can begin to flow freely.

The Spirit of Religion

This demonic spirit is likely the strongest in Satan's forces. It is this spirit that caused the religious leaders to condemn Jesus to the cross. At that time, the Pharisees and Sadducees were the most scripturally educated. They knew the scriptures better than anyone, yet, because of the spirit of religion, they were more concerned about what man thought, than what God thought. This caused them to be blind to the Messiah.

Church history shows that the spirit of religion resurfaced during the Dark Ages when the Bible was removed from the people and only priests could read and interpret it. The spirit of religion has been the root cause of many weird doctrines, practices, and cults that have spun off religious movements, and many holy wars.

Today we see the spirit of religion in our churches. Many pastors are more concerned about being people-sensitive, than about being God-sensitive. Like the Pharisees and Sadducees, they are still more concerned about the thoughts of men, than the thoughts of God.

It is the spirit of religion that also causes people to believe they have to earn God's favor. This spirit has created strong bondage for Christians in the area of finances, as many people now believe that God wants His people to be poor and totally reliant on Him. Well, they have the second part right, as God does want us to totally rely on Him. However, He does not want His children to be poor. He wants them to prosper. If you are still questioning that, go back to the list of prosperity scriptures earlier in the book.

In God's prosperity mindset, all we have to do is turn our life over to Jesus and make Him Lord of all parts of our life. Once we do that, we automatically become a child of God, which entitles us to the inheritance left to us when Jesus died (detailed in the New Testament). God's plan has no cost. Once you meet the qualifications (listed in Chapter 2), you are tapped in. At that point, the only thing that can stop the flow is sin, which brings us to the next demonic spirit, the spirit of mammon.

The Spirit of Mammon

This is also a very strong spirit. It is the spirit that motivated Judas Iscariot to turn on Jesus and hand Him over to the religious officials. In the Aramaic language, which was the language spoken by Jesus, mammon means "riches." According to the Catholic Encyclopedia, mammon was commonly regarded as a deity in the Middle Ages. John Milton in "Paradise Lost", depicts the spirit Mammon in heaven, forever looking down at the streets of gold, rather than up at God. After the rebellion in heaven, Mammon is relegated to hell with Lucifer. In De Plancy's "Dictionnaire Infernal", Mammon is mentioned as Hell's ambassador to England and equated with Lucifer, Satan, Beelzebub, and Nebuchadnezzar. Eastons Bible Dictionary defines Mammon as "a Chaldee or Syriac word meaning wealth or riches; also, by personification, the god of riches." According to the Oxford English Dictionary, Mammon is the name in the Bible of a demon who represents the sin of avarice (extreme greed for riches). By medieval times, it had become the proper name for the devil of covetousness. Lastly, the Reader's Digest Encyclopedic Dictionary defines mammon as, "Riches regarded as an evil influence and ignoble goal. Worldliness; avarice. The personification of riches, avarice and worldly gain."

So often, in the church, we hear money referred to as mammon. This is another one of the devil's deceptions. Mammon is not money. It's not even wealth or riches, as much as it is the state of spirit. Mammon is when wealth becomes the reason a person does everything in life. Mammon is a false god that takes our attention away from the true God. The first commandment says, "I am the Lord thy God; Thou shalt have no other gods before me." Mammon is one of those other gods. Do not overlook this powerful demonic spirit that is attempting to destroy your life daily.

Check yourself to see if you are under the influence of the spirit of mammon. Are any of these true:

Have you purchased a house or car that was more expensive than you could afford just to create status?

Do you purchase clothing based on what other people will think?

Do you think about money more than you do God?

40

Have you made job or career changes, totally based on money?

Do you travel for show?

When you give, do you make sure others know?

Do you talk about current or future wealth more than you do about God?

If your answer was yes to any of these questions, then you are being influenced by the spirit of mammon. The Pharisees made a public show of their giving; often changing larger forms of money into smaller coins, so that they would make a bigger noise when poured into the offering container. For many years, people have given large sums to the church so they could be recognized and have influence. These people were all practicing mammonism – devotion to the pursuit of wealth or riches (also known as materialism). Americans are the worst of the "mammonists," as our whole society is built on the pursuit of wealth.

The spirit of mammon manifests itself in many ways. Here are a few:

1. **Blocking the flow of finances to God's people** – the spirit of mammon causes people to become greedy, resulting in hoarding. Satan uses the spirit of mammon to create human reservoirs. These are people who take the financial wealth given to them and keep it for themselves and for their benefit alone. They become like a body of water without an outlet (the Dead Sea or a stagnant pond are examples). Water that sits stagnant becomes dirty and smelly. It is filled with disease and all kinds of evil things. People who are blinded by the spirit of mammon, may flourish for a time, but destruction soon follows. It's not the wealth that causes destruction, but rather the "mammon mindset" that keeps them away from God, that destroys.

2. **Corrupting the flow of finances** – sometimes even flowing waters can be bad. For example, the mighty Amazon River is one of the most polluted bodies of water on

earth. Why? Because of waste that is constantly pouring into the river. The spirit of mammon tries to do the same thing with our financial river. It influences people with greed to create a higher perception of need for material things. This results in people using credit to obtain things now, instead of waiting until they could afford them. Greed will also often result in gambling, whether physically through the Lottery or a casino or by jumping into risky business ventures or scams, because they have the potential for a quick return.

The spirit of mammon loves to use interest to bind people. Interest or usury (as it is referred to in the Bible) is abominable to God. Leviticus 25:36 says, "Take no usury or interest from him, but fear your God . . ." Verse 37 continues by saying, "You shall not lend him your money for usury . . ." Proverbs 28:8 says, "One who increases his possessions by usury and extortion, gathers it for him who will pity the poor." Ezekiel 22:12 says, ". . . 'you take usury and increase; you have made profit from your neighbors by extortion, and have forgotten Me,' says the Lord God." It is very clear that God does not like usury or interest. Why? God hates usury because the company that is loaning the money with interest (banks, mortgage and credit card companies) becomes a false God. Interest cuts off the flow of faith. When we depend on financial institutions and credit, God doesn't get a chance to grow our faith.

Gambling is another of mammon's favorite tools to bind people. We used to think of gambling as something you did in Las Vegas or Reno, but now, at least here in Washington State, there are casinos popping up all over the place. Then there is the Lottery, which has become an institution in every state. Have you ever made the statement, "When I win the lottery . . .?" If so, then you were being motivated by the spirit of mammon at that moment. Gambling is another abomination to God. Proverbs 10:2 says, "Ill-gotten gains do not profit..." Remember earlier when you learned that the devil is looking for people to become reservoirs – one of the greatest examples of this is Las Vegas. It is literally a money reservoir in the middle of the desert, full of all kinds of evil. Satan will dump money on people, to destroy their lives. We know of one young couple that won 12 million dollars in the lottery. They immediately bought a very expensive new home with a huge monthly mortgage. Next were his and hers luxury cars. Then they bought new wardrobes and went on exotic vacations. Since they were receiving their lottery winnings over a 20-year period, they began to borrow against future years. Things got bad and a year later they were divorced and bankrupt.

God doesn't dump money on His kids. He builds our character first. 3 John 2 says, "Beloved, I pray that you may prosper in all things and be in health, just as your soul prospers."

Abraham understood this principle well. He was a faithful steward. He knew that God was his source, so when human kings offered him the opportunity for wealth, he turned them down, so that no man could say that he made Abraham wealthy. Abraham understood that God was building up his character through work. Proverbs 10:4 says, "Lazy hands make a man poor, but diligent hands bring wealth." When we are in God's will and His plan, our diligent work will bring divine prosperity.

The spirit of mammon is strong in the United States. We must begin to plead the Blood of Jesus over our country, state, city, community, church, and home. We must depend on God for our source of finances, not the devices of the devil and his demonic forces.

How to Develop a Divine Prosperity Mindset

Now that you have a better understanding of how the enemy works, it's important that you understand how your mind works and how to develop a prosperity mindset. There are six stages of the thought process:

1. **Pictures** – our brain sees everything in picture form. For example, if someone told you to think about a pink elephant, you would see a pink elephant in your mind. You wouldn't see the words pink and elephant. In your brain you have millions of pictures stored and you pull them up thousands of times every day. Since your mind operates in pictures, what does prosperity look like to you? By reading and meditating over the scriptures, you can make sure that you have a proper picture of prosperity. That is the first step in developing a divine prosperity mindset.

2. **Paradigms** – The American Century Dictionary defines paradigm as, an "example or pattern." They can also be unwritten rules and assumptions that govern how we view things. All the pictures in your mind come together like the single frames of a motion picture to create your paradigms. As you change the frames, you change your paradigms. Most likely, you have paradigms about prosperity. Unless you have already spent a great deal of time reading the Bible, studying what God has to say about prosperity, then your paradigm has been dramatically influenced by what the world says about prosperity. If you have grown up in the church, perhaps you have even been subject to the poverty mindset that has been prevalent in the church for decades. It is critical that you read, study, and meditate over the Word of God, so that the new pictures in your mind can create a new divine paradigm.

3. **Programs** – Much like the computer on your desk or at home, your mind runs programs. No, you don't have to load software, but your mind does run programs based on your paradigms. Your brain automatically collects data, provided by your paradigms, to set your ways of thinking into a program that will continue to run unconsciously. We have many ways of thinking or "mind sets" that may or may not be true, based on what information our brain has collected and how we interpret that information. This is why the Bible tells us to "be ye transformed by the renewing of your mind" (Romans 12:2). The ways of the world are always

diametrically opposed to the ways of God, particularly when it comes to the subject of money.

As your paradigms about money and prosperity change, so will the programs. You will begin to process differently. Perhaps you have always been somewhat pessimistic about finances and you'll find yourself knowing that prosperity is on its way to you. As your programs begin to change, you are halfway to a divine prosperity mindset.

4. **Expectations** – Your expectations have been created by the programs that run in your brain. Expectations will determine your level of prosperity. As you move through a change in your thought process about prosperity, your expectations will rise to a new level. Proverbs 23:7 says, "For as he thinks in his heart, so is he." Matthew 9:29 says, "According to your faith, let it be to you." As you expect more, you open the door for God to give you more.

5. **Actions** – What you do is based on your expectations. If you are seriously seeking and serving God, then your expectations will be high, because you know the promises of God. As you expect more and are listening to God's instructions, you will change your actions. Perhaps you will do some things you have never done before – give more, save more, invest more, or maybe start your own side business. The greater your expectations, the greater your actions.

6. **Results** – From your actions, you will always get results. If your actions have been God-directed, your results will be excellent. On the other hand, if your actions are you-directed, then you will have mixed results. In either case, you get results. Once you have a result, it's time to analyze it and determine if your thought process is in line with God's. What many people try to do is ignore the first four steps and simply change their results by changing their actions. If you attempt to do it this way, you will have limited results because you will not be able to maintain any actions that don't line up with your expectations, programs,

paradigms, and pictures. You will sooner or later revert back to the "old way of doing things" and get the same old results. If you aren't getting the results you want, it's time to go back to the beginning and check your pictures, paradigms, programs, and expectations. Each time you do this, you will get closer to a true divine prosperity mindset.

The key to this whole process is to read, study, and meditate on the Word of God every day. Psalm 1:1-3 says, "Blessed is the man who does not walk in the counsel of the wicked or stand in the way of sinners or sit in the seat of mockers. But his delight is in the law of the Lord, and on His law, he meditates day and night. He is like a tree planted by streams of water, which yields its fruit in season and whose leaf does not wither. Whatever he does prospers." Would you like everything you do to prosper? Get your thought processes in line with God by reading and meditating over the Word of God.

Differences between Materialism and Divine Prosperity

Since you now have a good understanding of your thought process, it's time to make sure that you have the right pictures planted about prosperity. In this section, you will learn the differences between materialism (the world's prosperity plan) and divine prosperity (God's prosperity plan).

Materialism - The American Heritage Dictionary defines materialism as, "the attitude that physical well-being and worldly possessions constitute the greatest good and highest value in life." You've seen the bumper sticker, "He who dies with the most toys wins." This is how many people view prosperity. It's completely linear and limited to this one life on earth. Our world totally revolves around materialism, so the influences on our lives are very heavy. Materialism is an abomination to God, because materialists are relying solely on their own abilities to create wealth. There is no room for God in materialism. However, there is also no room for materialists in God's eternal world. To the materialist, money is god and as Jesus said in Luke 16:13, "No servant can serve two masters. Either he will hate the one and love the other, or he will be devoted to the one and despise the other. You cannot serve both God and money." Materialism is a tool of the devil that is driven by our own human pride. Satan uses it to keep us from God, because he knows the amazing treasures that God has for us, if we tap into His divine prosperity plan.

Divine Prosperity – Quite often, in order to find out what something is, we have to find out what it is not. This is the case when we begin to try to understand divine prosperity. Isaiah 55:9 says, "As the heavens are higher than the earth, so are my ways higher than your ways and my thoughts than your thoughts." God's divine plan is impossible to understand on our own, but all things are possible with God. Materialism is based on self-reliance, but divine prosperity is based on God-reliance. Materialism is selfish by nature, whereas divine prosperity is self-less. Materialism requires you to build yourself up, often at the expense of others; divine prosperity requires you to give up your selfish ways and serve others. In materialism, the more you keep the better you are; in divine prosperity, the more you give, the better you are. Divine prosperity is the polar opposite of materialism in every way, except the result – prosperity. The biggest key to divine prosperity is obedience to God. Abraham, Isaac, Jacob, David, and Solomon, all understood this principle and God prospered them abundantly. God is abundance; He walks on streets of gold and owns everything in the universe. Doesn't it make a lot more sense to get close to Him and learn how to tap into His plan?

Abundance Mentality

Jesus said, "The thief comes only to steal and kill and destroy, I came that they may have life, and have it abundantly." (John 10:10) Jesus had an abundance

47

mentality, just like His Father. Since we are also God's children, we too should learn to have an abundance mentality. Unfortunately, we live in a "my slice of the pie" world, where everyone is just trying to get their slice of the one pie that they think is available. So many people are wasting their lives trying to increase the size of their piece by working harder. This is such limited mentality and will keep them in the proverbial "rat race" forever. Have you ever seen a caged rat? Typically they have an exercise wheel and if you've ever observed a rat, you will notice that it will run as fast as it can on the wheel and then get out and look around (as if it were going to be in a different place). This is the way people are living their lives. They are running on that wheel of life every day – running as hard as they can and at the end of each day, week, month, and year, they look around and realize they haven't really gone anywhere. Oh sure, they are making more money, living in a bigger house, and driving a nicer car, but for what? They still feel empty and unfulfilled.

Satan is the author of the rat race. He has always hated human beings and as it says in John 10:10, he comes only to steal, kill, and destroy. If the rat keeps us running like rats, then we are just like him and can never be like God. Even born-again believers are caught in the rat race. Although, the devil knows he can't have their soul, he can keep them so busy pursuing the "American Dream" that they don't have time to really get close to God and realize that He has a much better plan.

God is the author of the world. He created everything, which means that He operates with a creative paradigm. In God's plan there are plenty of pies to go around – in fact, you don't have to be limited to your slice, you can have the whole pie and it won't even affect anyone else's share. God lives in an unlimited world and when we enter into His plan, so do we. Remember that those of us who have accepted Jesus into our hearts and made Him Lord and Savior of our lives, are now part of God's family. Jesus came to earth to die and give us our family inheritance. Ephesians 1:13-14 says, "And you also were included in Christ when you heard the word of truth, the gospel of your salvation. Having believed, you were marked in him with a seal, the promised Holy Spirit, who is a deposit guaranteeing our inheritance . . ." According to Matthew 11:27, all things were committed to Jesus by the Father. Since we are inheriting all of what Jesus had (as co-heirs with Him), we have access to all that the Father has and that is everything. The key is to get into a mindset for receiving.

The next thing we need to understand is that the world's prosperity plan is limited by physical and economic laws, whereas God's plan is unlimited. Let's look at a few examples:

1. **Jesus feeds the 5,000** (Matthew 14:13-21) – Jesus had been administering healing to a large crowd for some time and evening was approaching. The disciples suggested that Jesus send the crowd back home to eat, before it got too late. Jesus replied by telling the disciples to feed them. Unfortunately, they were still operating with a worldly mentality of lack and could not see how over 5,000 people could be fed with what little food they had and not enough money to buy enough additional food. Jesus, who operated with an abundance mentality, took what they had, five loaves of bread and two fish, and fed the whole group, which likely numbered between 10,000 and 15,000 people (in those days they only counted the men which numbered 5,000). Not only was there plenty of food for everyone, but there were twelve basketfuls of broken pieces left over. God showed that He is a God of more than enough.

In the world's prosperity plan, what Jesus did would be impossible, as it is limited to what is available in the physical realm. Physically they had five loaves of bread and two fish, which could not feed all of the people. However, in God's realm, the spiritual realm, there is an unlimited supply of food. Because Jesus had spent so much time with the Father,

He knew how to reach beyond the physical realm and into the spiritual realm, thus opening them to an unlimited amount of food. It would not have mattered whether there were 10,000 or 10 million people, all would have gotten fed. Now, let's look at another example showing the difference between the world's plan and God's plan.

2. **Money from a fish** (Matthew 17:24-27) – The tax collectors approached Jesus and Peter, asking if they were going to pay the tax. Jesus saw this as an opportunity to teach Peter about the source of his income. Normally, Peter would have thought of worldly ways to get the money, but Jesus showed him that God is his source. He sent Peter off to catch a fish and told him to look in the fish's mouth. Peter did as he was told and found a gold coin, which was given to the tax collector to pay the taxes for both of them.

Again, in the physical realm of the world, this was an impossible situation. Who would even think to go look in a fish's mouth for a coin? Because Jesus understood the connection between the physical and spiritual realms, He was able to draw from the spiritual realm into the physical realm and produce the coin. God is your source as well and He has an unlimited supply of money for each of His children. If He can produce a coin from a fish's mouth, surely he can take care of your financial situation. The key is learning how to reach into the spiritual realm and pull what God has already marked for you, into the physical realm. Now, let's look at an example of someone who truly understood the difference between things that have worldly value and those that have eternal value.

3. **Costly Perfume** (Mark 14:3-11) – While Jesus was sitting in the home of Simon the Leper, Mary (of Mary and Martha) broke a jar of very expensive perfume and began to pour it on Jesus' head. She was immediately rebuked by the disciples, particularly Judas (who was the treasurer). Jesus immediately rebuked them and said that what she had done was good. Jesus was not concerned about the cost of the

perfume, because He was operating out of abundance. Mary obviously understood this principle as well. However, the disciples were still operating with a "lack" mentality.

Jesus was fully connected with the Father's prosperity plan. He was able to take something in the natural, like 5 loaves of bread and 2 fish, and reach into the supernatural realm to multiply them and feed over 10,000 people. He had learned to funnel from the supernatural to the natural. We too can learn how to do this, but we have to get our eyes off the natural and on to the supernatural. Matthew 6:33 says, "But seek first his kingdom and righteousness, and all these things will be given to you as well." Everything God has is available to us, if we just get our eyes focused on Him and off the world and its limitations.

Expand Your Financial Vision

Our worldly paradigm causes our financial vision to look like a funnel. God is pouring His abundance into the large open top, but our worldly paradigms of lack, constrict the blessings down to a narrow opening. God's plan looks more like a large tube. God is pouring His blessings into the large top and it flows through the same size opening into our lives. The key here is that you must learn to expand your financial vision to receive the fullness of God's prosperity.

Right now, your financial vision probably is limited to a pay check every week, two weeks, or once a month. Maybe you also receive some interest on savings or dividends from investments. If you have been financially shrewd, you might even have a secondary source of income, like real estate investments or a home business. No matter what your current situation, it's not even close to what His plan looks like.

Imagine checks for thousands of dollars arriving in your mailbox or being handed to you every day. How about money that just shows up in your account? A husband and wife who graduated from the first God's Prosperity Plan course (which is available on cassette and in a video facilitated format at www.truthandgracebooks.com) had this happen. The husband and his wife learned how to expand their financial vision and tap into God's prosperity plan. One day he stopped by his bank to use the ATM to get some cash. When he looked at the receipt, he noticed that his balance was too high - $10,000 too high. When he checked with the bank, he found that the balance was correct. Someone had deposited $10,000 into his bank account. It turned out that the government owed him some money from his time in the military years earlier and deposited it directly into his account, including the interest. Ten years later the government literally tracked him down and then without any notice, deposited $10,000 into his account. That has to be God! When you are operating in God's prosperity plan, sometimes money just shows up.

Another example was a person who had been in the church all her life. She attended services every time they were held, was in the choir, volunteered for various programs, and tithed faithfully. However, she had never fully understood the principles of God's prosperity plan. After gaining a better understanding of God's promises, she expanded her financial vision and started calling on God's prosperity promises. Within 24 hours she received a letter indicating that she and her sister were the owners of some stock that their deceased father had purchased many years earlier. It turned out that the stock was worth over $30,000!

You will learn more about tithing later, but in Malachi 3:10, God tells us that if we tithe, He will "throw open the floodgates of heaven and pour out so much blessing that you will not have room enough for it." I (Rod) believe these to be the same floodgates that God used to flood the earth in Noah's day. However, instead of water, he's going to flow blessing into your life. Imagine having so much financial blessing coming into your life that you can't give it away quickly enough to keep up! That's God's prosperity plan.

All you need to do is expand your financial vision to meet His.

So, how do we expand our financial vision? Here are several ways:

1. **Look Beyond Yourself** – Most people are operating with a "we four and no more" paradigm. This means that they are providing for their family and no more. If you are going to tap into God's plan, you must look beyond your own needs and those of your family to the needs in your extended family, church, community and throughout the world. In Matthew 25:31-46, Jesus teaches us about this principle in the parable of the sheep and goats. Here he tells us that at the time of the final judgment, the sheep (those who followed Jesus, the great Shepherd) will be separated from the goats (those who did it the world's way). The difference Jesus gives is that the sheep fed the hungry, gave drink to the thirsty, invited strangers in, clothed those who were without clothing, and looked after the sick. In other words, they looked past their own circumstances to those of the people around them. We too must do this. Jesus told us to love each other, as He loves us. It's time to get your eyes off your circumstances (no matter how bad they seem) and begin to look for ways you can help others. Once you open your eyes, you will find many programs that feed and clothe the homeless, take in runaways, aid pregnant teens, help the abused, counsel the suicidal, and more.

Use the gifts that God has given you to reach out to people in need and your circumstances will rapidly change for the better. Pastor Tim: "When I was in Bogota, Columbia, I found over 6 million people, many of whom were homeless. I gave to beggars, when others said that they would just spend the money on drugs – I gave anyway." We are not to be the judge; that's God's job. When you are approached by someone in need, give of your money or time, and God will reward you, because He takes how we treat the rest of His children personally!

If the church does not take care of the people in need, who will? So often, we Christians, leave that up to the government. So far, they have done a fair job, but we have done a poor job. God calls us to be His Hands and Feet. What are we doing with them? Most of us are struggling with not enough or just enough time and money to take care of ourselves, much less anyone else. Once again, this is scarcity mentality and not of God. Later in the book, you will learn more about the law of sowing and reaping, but briefly, if you don't sow, you can't reap. If you are living paycheck-to-paycheck, it could be because you aren't sowing enough. Think about a farm. If the farmer doesn't sow any seed, he doesn't reap a crop. The basis of the law of sowing and reaping is that we receive in proportion to our giving. In Luke 6:38 Jesus says, "Give and it will be given to you. A good measure, pressed down, shaken together and running over, will be poured into your lap. For with the measure you use, it will be measured to you." How big is your measure? If your measure of sowing is by the teaspoon, don't expect God to multiply it into truckloads. The more you sow, the more you reap.

2. **Read the Word Daily** – The devil doesn't want your financial vision expanded, so he is going to do everything possible to see you up to your ears in alligators. The only way to get out of the swamp is to read, study, and meditate on God's Word EVERY day. As you read the great prosperity promises, God can reveal His heart and His plan for you. Joshua 1:8 says, "This Book of the Law shall not depart from your mouth, but you shall meditate on it day and night, that you may observe to do according to all that is written in it. For then you will make your way prosperous, and then you will have good success." Deuteronomy 29:9 says, "Therefore keep the words of this covenant, and do them, that you may prosper in all you do." You can learn about the covenants by studying the old and new covenants (testaments).

By reading the Word daily, we are seeking God. 2 Chronicles 26:5 says, "He set himself to seek God in the days of Zechariah, who instructed him in the things of God; and as long as he sought the Lord, God made him prosper." Just like human fathers, God loves it when His children earnestly seek Him through reading His Word. Also, just like human fathers, He likes to reward His children with good gifts. Jesus addressed this in Matthew 7:11 when He said, "If you, though you are evil, know how to give good gifts to your children, how much more will your Father in heaven give good gifts to those who ask Him!" When we read His Word every day, we are asking for Him to bestow good gifts upon us.

Through reading and meditating on the Word, we gain spiritual wisdom that enables us to see more clearly into the spiritual realm. God is wisdom and from wisdom comes power. "To God belong wisdom and power, counsel and understanding are His." (Job 12:13) He gives wisdom to those He chooses and those who ask. When given the opportunity to ask anything of God, Solomon chose wisdom. God gave him wisdom beyond anyone else and also rewarded him with wealth and health. How do we gain wisdom from the Word? The first step is fear (awe, reverence, respect) of the Lord. "The fear of the Lord is the beginning of wisdom; all who follow His precepts have good understanding." (Psalm 111:10) To those who fear Him, He gives wisdom. "For the Lord gives wisdom, and from His mouth comes knowledge and understanding." (Proverbs 2:6) God gives wisdom to those who read and follow His Word. "Get wisdom, get understanding, do not forget My words or swerve from them." (Proverbs 4:5) Wisdom cannot be learned, only given to you by God. "To the man who pleases Him, God gives wisdom, knowledge, and happiness. . ." (Ecclesiastes 2:26) "If any of you lacks wisdom, he should ask God, who gives generously to all without finding fault, and it will be given to him." Seek God in the scriptures every day. Ask and you will be given wisdom and knowledge of God's prosperity plan.

3. **Gain A Spiritual Perspective** – In our opinion, we are in the end times and because we are, God is speeding things up. In the final days, the Bible prophesies that there will be a great wealth transfer. The wealth of the wicked has been laid up for the righteous. All of those who have been faithful, with what God has given them, will be entrusted with great wealth and become the channels through which God sends the money necessary to fund a great worldwide revival. According to Joel 2, during that time the Lord will "repay you for the years the locusts have eaten. . ." What the enemy has taken from you and your family will be repaid and there will be abundance. This great harvest is near for those who are sowing. Are you sowing into God's Kingdom or are you sowing into the world? Understand that it may look bad now and that evil people are prospering, but the righteous will prosper in the end.

It is also important for us to remember that the things of this world will soon pass away. There has never been a dead millionaire who took his/her wealth to the grave. However, Jesus taught us to lay up treasures in heaven that will last for eternity. We are all focused on a very short earthly time line, whereas God has an eternal focus. He's looking at the grand plan and guiding those who seek Him to understand that the things we do on earth also have an eternal result. If we get in line with His plan and take the time to develop a prosperity mindset by renewing our minds to the truth of God's Word, we will truly have the mind of Christ.

We will then be able to see the big picture similar to the way God does. We will have a greater understanding of how the physical and spiritual realms work together. We will no longer rely on the world's sources for our prosperity, but rather will rely on God to bring prosperity from the store-rooms in heaven into our life, through our faith. Then we will enjoy prosperity in this earthly life, while we are laying up treasures in heaven for our eternal life.

Chapter Three Discussion Questions

1. What is the spirit of religion and how does it affect Christians?

2. What is the spirit of mammon and how does it affect Christians?

3. Why is God so against interest (usury)? Gambling?

5. What are the six stages of the thought process? Discuss each stage.

6. What are the differences between materialism and divine prosperity?

7. Describe and discuss "abundance mentality."

8. Do you really believe that God fed 5,000+ with the loaves and fish? Discuss.

9. How did Mary's waste of expensive perfume show abundance mentality?

10. Quickly write your financial vision and share with the group.

11. What does it mean to "look beyond yourself" to expand your financial vision?

12. Discuss the need to read God's Word every day and make a plan to do so.

Four

Principles of
Sowing and Reaping

Chapter 4

Principles of Sowing and Reaping

Farmers have understood this principle for thousands of years. They sow seed into good ground and reap a harvest of fruit, vegetables, or grain. The more they sow, the more they reap. In this chapter, you will learn about the spiritual law of sowing and reaping. It is one of the most powerful of the spiritual laws. You will learn how to sow God's promises into your heart; the most effective ways to sow your financial seeds; the things that will block the flow of God's blessings when sowing; how to recognize good spiritual ground; the purpose and power of tithing; the keys to giving; a comparison of the world's way and God's way; an introduction to the spiritual laws and how sowing and reaping fits; and a clear picture of God's plan for sowing and reaping.

Sow God's Promises into Your Heart

We reap what we sow in all aspects of our life. If we sow into disobedience, as Adam and Eve did, then we will reap disaster and spiritual death. Galatians 6:7-8 says, "Do not be deceived: God cannot be mocked. A man reaps what he sows. The one who sows to please his sinful nature, from that nature will reap destruction . . ." Self-focused decisions and plans put God in second place. When you sow into the world's system, you can only reap the world's harvest. God cannot bless that process. Acts 8:18 shows us a great example of someone who wanted to sow into the Kingdom, but do it his (the world's) way. Simon, who was a sorcerer, saw that the Holy Spirit was given when the apostles laid hands on someone. He offered them money to lay hands on him, so that he might receive the power to lay hands on others and have them receive the baptism of the Holy Spirit. In verse 20, Peter answers by saying, "May your money perish with you, because you thought you could buy the gift of God with money! You have no part or share in this ministry, because your heart is not right before God. Repent of this wickedness and pray to the Lord. Perhaps He will forgive you for having such a thought in your heart. For I see that you are full of bitterness and captive to sin." Peter was telling him (and us) that we should be sowing into the Spirit always and never into the ways of the world.

When we sow to please the Spirit, we are God-focused, but how do you sow to the Spirit? Put Christ first in everything. There is a great book that teaches this powerful principal – In His Steps by Charles Sheldon. You can find it at www.truthandgracebooks.com for just a few dollars. In this book a whole town begins to operate their lives by first asking the question, "What would Jesus do?" This of course is where the "WWJD?" movement was birthed. We would all do well to live our lives that way; by making all decisions based on what Jesus would do. How can we know what Jesus would do? Study His life in the Bible. Get in the habit of reading the Bible every day and you will have a greater understanding of how the Father, Son, and Holy Spirit operate. Again, as it says in Joshua 1:8, "Do not let this Book of the Law depart from your mouth; meditate on it day and night, so that you may be careful to do everything written in it. Then you will be prosperous and successful." Plant God's promises firmly into your heart by reading and meditating on His Word every day.

Remember what Jesus taught us in Matthew 6:33: To seek God's Kingdom and His Righteousness first and everything else would fall into line. If you are seeking the world – materialism, then you are moving in the opposite direction from God. A second way to sow into the Spirit is through prayer. Not a quick prayer before meals or at bedtime, but rather dedicated time each day where you focus on God. Unfortunately, most people think that prayer means asking God for stuff. Learn to just spend time getting to know God. Ask Him questions and then be quiet enough to hear His still small voice in your heart. The more you practice, the better you will get at shutting out the noise of the world and opening your spiritual ears, so you can hear God clearly. After all, He is the creator of the universe who is "all-knowing;" doesn't it make sense to get clear direction from Him? When you spend time with God, you develop a relationship that will last for eternity and that pleases Him and will help you to tap into His prosperity plan.

For many years I (Rod) was away from the Lord. I studied the ways of the world and made up my own plans; which failed miserably every time. When I came back to the Lord, I was still operating in the world's plan, so I would develop plans and then ask God to bless them. Again, these plans did not produce the results I was hoping for. As I grew in my relationship with God, I began to trust Him to develop the plans. I would seek His direction and would not move forward until I had clear direction. The results have been amazing. Now the trust level is so high that God often allows me to develop my own plans, which He tweaks to meet His needs. It's a process that requires mutual trust and the only way you can build that kind of trust is to invest time with God.

When we sow into the Spirit, we also sow good things into our heart. Since our heart is a garden, it will grow whatever is planted; both good and bad. The devil wants you to plant bad seeds into your heart, so you will be ineffective for God. That's why Satan has perverted things like television, movies, newspapers, and the Internet. Now don't get the wrong idea, these mediums are not all bad, but they are avenues that the enemy uses to pass on his bad news and pollute our hearts. So guard your heart. Proverbs 4:23 says, "Above all else, guard your heart, for it is the wellspring of life." Out of your heart will flow whatever you plant, so be acutely aware of what you are allowing to be planted.

One way to assure that you are planting good seeds is to plant the Word of God. There are many, many scriptures about prosperity in the Bible. Here are a few that you can plant into your heart garden:

Deuteronomy 28:11: "The Lord will grant you abundant prosperity – in the fruit of your womb, the young of your livestock and the crops of your ground – in the land He swore to your forefathers to give you."

Psalm 35:27: "Let them shout for joy and be glad, who favor My righteous cause, and let them say continually, "Let the Lord be magnified, who has pleasure in the prosperity of His servant."

Proverbs 10:22: "The blessing of the Lord brings wealth, and He adds no trouble in it."

Isaiah 48:15: "I, even I, have spoken, yes, I have called him, I have brought him, and his way will prosper."

Isaiah 52:13: "Behold My servant will prosper, he will be high and lifted up and greatly exalted."

2 Chronicles 26:5: "He continued to seek God in the days of Zechariah, who had understanding through the vision of God; and as long as he sought the Lord, God prospered him."

Deuteronomy 29:9: "Carefully follow the terms of this covenant, so that you may prosper in everything you do."

Deuteronomy 30:9: "Then the Lord your God will prosper your abundantly in all the work of your hand, in the offspring of your body and in the offspring of your cattle and in the produce of your ground, for the Lord will again rejoice over you for good, just as He rejoiced over your fathers."

Proverbs 13:21: "Misfortune pursues the sinner, but prosperity is the reward of the righteous."

John 10:10: "The thief does not come except to steal, and to kill, and to destroy. I have come that they may have life, and that they may have it abundantly."

(You will find many more prosperity scriptures in Appendix B at the end of this book)

Is poverty or indebtedness abundant life? Of course not! It's not what God had in mind when He planted Adam and Eve in paradise – giving them dominion over everything on the earth. That's abundance! Is there any doubt that God wants His kids (including you) to be prosperous? If you still have doubt, stop reading and go back to the scriptures and spend some time reading and meditating over them. God will use those to plant good seeds into your heart. Once they have been firmly planted into your heart, God can begin to do His work through you.

In the beginning, God spoke the universe into existence (Genesis 1). He wants to do the same thing in your life. He wants to speak prosperity into your life, but He can only do it by the spirit of faith that dwells within you. In 2 Corinthians 4:13 the apostle Paul writes, "It is written, 'I believed; therefore I have spoken.' With that same spirit of faith we also believe and therefore speak. . ." If you are a born-again believer and follower of Christ, then God has given you the spirit of faith to speak prosperity into existence in your life. Daily, repeat God's promises out loud and into your life. The more you do this, the more your faith will increase. It is your faith that God uses as a conduit to bring prosperity from the spiritual realm into your physical world. The stronger your faith, the bigger the potential blessing, so work daily to build up your faith. The Bible says that we are to build up our faith through hearing the message of the Word of God. Reading and meditating over the Bible every day will enable you to hear the messages that God has specifically for you, which will build up your faith.

No matter how hard you try to keep the bad seeds out of your garden they will grow. Just like the garden in your yard, you're going to need to weed it daily. Satan will use the things of the world to plant promise-choking weeds in your garden. If you leave them, they will slowly choke out the dreams and plans for prosperity that God has for you. To weed your garden, ask the Lord to search your heart daily to bring up unrepented sin. When those come to the surface, don't allow the devil to get you wallowing in the sin, just wholeheartedly repent and move on. Psalm 51:10 says, "Create in me a pure heart, O God, and renew a steadfast spirit within me." Pray daily that God will reveal the weeds that are in your garden, so that you can dig them out with your shovel of repentance.

Here is what you should be sowing into your garden:

Three rows of Peas – peace of mind, peace of heart, peace of soul.

Four rows of Squash – squash gossip, indifference, grumbling, and selfishness.

Four rows of Lettuce – lettuce be faithful, kind, happy, and really love one another.

Three rows of Turnips – turnip for service, to help each other and the music and dance.

Four rows of Thyme – time for the Lord, rest, fun, and you.

(Author unknown)

Sow the promises of God into your heart, because if you don't, the devil will sow the curses of the world and you will struggle financially all of your life. God has created a seed system. In 1st Corinthians 3:6 Paul writes, "I planted the seed, Apollos watered it, but God made it grow." In some versions of the Bible it says, "but God gave the increase." Here's how it works: God gives you seeds (money) to plant; you plant your seeds into good ground (ministry); the ministry waters the seed; and God provides the growth or increase for both you and the ministry where you planted the seeds. Plus, as you faithfully proceed through the sowing process, He will provide more seed. 2 Corinthians 9:10 says, "Now He who supplies seed to the sower and bread for food will also supply and increase your store of seed and will enlarge the harvest of your righteousness." So, sow your seeds and God will give you more.

Sounds easy right? Wrong! Satan doesn't want you to plant your seed, so he will create hindrances. Here are some of the most common hindrances:

1. People hold on to their seed (money) and never plant it. The world teaches to "save for a rainy day." The devil wants you to hold on to the seed God has given you, just in case something happens and you need it. God says, trust me, have faith, plant your seed and I will provide for your needs.

2. People eat the seed God meant to be sowed. God gives us enough seed to take care of our needs and the rest is to be sowed into Kingdom pursuits. Unfortunately, most people overspend and use credit to live beyond their means. If this isn't affecting you now, it will eventually keep you from tithing and giving. Make sure you are living within the means that God has provided and that you are sowing the seeds He provided for planting into your prosperity plan. He will use the seed to cause increase, which will result in a larger harvest. You will then have more to live on and more to give. This is a continuous upward cycle, if you do your part.

3. People sow their seeds into bad ground. In Matthew 13:3-8, the parable of the sower, Jesus teaches us what happens if our seed is planted in bad ground:

"Then He spoke many things to them in parables, saying: 'Behold, a sower went out to sow. And as he sowed, some seed fell by the wayside; and the birds came and devoured them. Some fell on stony places, where they did not have much earth; and they immediately sprang up because they had no depth of earth; But when the sun was up they were scorched and because they had no root they withered away. And some fell among thorns, and the thorns sprang up and choked them.'" Here we can clearly see that if we are not careful in our planting, that our seed will produce no harvest. If you plant your seeds in worldly things – investments, schemes and scams, gambling or even material things like cars, clothes, and trips, instead of planting your seeds into the Kingdom, then you are hindering God's plan to prosper you. Now, don't get the idea that you have to give it all away. God is calling you to give what He has given you to give and to eat what He has given you to eat. You hinder His plan, when you misuse the seed He has given you to plant.

4. People don't believe that God blesses. God's prosperity plan works by faith. If you continue to tip God out of duty, then He cannot bless you with prosperity. Jesus said that if you have faith, the size of a mustard seed, you could move that mountain (of debt). What seems impossible to you is not impossible to God. Believe that God can not only remove the debt, but also bring you into a level of prosperity that you have never imagined, and He can begin to work.

These hindrances are keeping Christians broke, living paycheck-to-paycheck, deeply in debt and unable to finance the gospel. If Christians don't finance the gospel, who will? Satan has a huge investment into the world's prosperity plan; it's time that we loose the flow of God's abundance into the world, so that people can see who the real King is!

There are also some things that people do that block the flow of God's blessings. This is called self-sabotage. It will happen quite often, just as God is starting to work or as the prosperity is really flowing. Here are a few of the most common ways you can sabotage God's efforts:

1. **Try to figure out God's plan for you.** Isaiah 55:9 says, "For as the heavens are higher than the earth, so are My ways higher than your ways and My thoughts than your thoughts." God is all knowing and we are not, so quit trying to figure out His plan. Our pea brains will never be able to

fully understand what He is doing. Plus, He doesn't call us to understand, just to be obedient. He doesn't want us relying on our own understanding and abilities, so He doesn't give us the whole plan. He gives us small pieces and then expects us to walk forward, trusting fully in Him.

2. **Inconsistency.** Christians spend years sowing into the world and reaping destruction and then they sow into the Kingdom for a few weeks or months and expect everything to miraculously turn around. You reap what you sow. If you've been sowing into the world, you will continue to reap those negative benefits for a period of time. It takes some time to turn this around, so it's important that you consistently sow into God's Kingdom, then be patient and trust in God.

3. **Pride.** When things start going well, be careful to whom you give the credit. If you start taking any of the credit, you will block the flow of blessing quicker than anything else you can do. Proverbs 11:2 says, "When pride comes, then comes disgrace, but with humility comes wisdom." Proverbs 18:12 "Before his downfall a man's heart is proud, but humility comes before honor." Proverbs 29:23 "A man's pride brings him low, but a man of lowly spirit (humility) gains honor." Give God the credit, for there is nothing good without Him. Deuteronomy 8:18 says, "But remember the Lord your God, for it is He who gives you the ability to produce wealth, and so confirms His covenant, which He swore to your forefathers, as it is today." Take credit and the blessings will stop. Give God all the credit and the blessings will flow ever greater into your life.

4. **Taking the blessings for granted.** There will come a time when the flow of blessings gets very heavy and consistent. Don't take these blessings for granted. Never take God for granted. Deuteronomy 8:10-14 (NKJ) says, "When you have eaten and are full, then you shall bless the Lord your God for the good land which He has given you. Beware that you do not forget the Lord your God by not

keeping His commandments, His judgments, and His statutes which I command you today, and when your herds and your flocks multiply, and your silver and your gold are multiplied, and all that you have is multiplied; when your heart is lifted up, and you forget the Lord your God who brought you out of the land of Egypt, from the house of bondage." It's easy to ask God to bless you and then when the blessings are flowing, forget who blessed you. Remember to give God the credit and give thanks always.

5. **Misuse of the Blessings.** Christians always start with pure hearts, when they are poor and in need. Unfortunately, in many cases, as God begins to pour the blessings of prosperity into their lives, they begin to misuse the blessings. Sometimes the blessings don't come in the form we expect or as quickly as we had hoped and we begin to grumble. Moses had to deal with all of these issues with the Israelites. In Numbers 16:8-11, we read, "Moses also said to Korah, 'Now listen, you Levites! Isn't it enough for you that the God of Israel has separated you from the rest of the Israelite community and brought you near himself to do the work at the Lord's tabernacle and to stand before the community and minister to them? He has brought you and all your fellow Levites near himself, but now you are trying to get the priesthood too. It is against the Lord that you and all your followers have banded together. Who is Aaron that you should grumble against him?"

This happens so often in churches. People who give a lot of money or are selected for high lay positions, let it go to their head. They begin to try to throw their weight around by making demands. They try to control the Pastor's decisions. This is all misuse of the blessings of God and will surely block the flow of prosperity into your life.

Be aware of these hindrances, as Satan will try to tempt you in these areas. If the devil wasn't able to stop you from receiving God's blessings, then he will do everything possible to get you to do things that will either hinder or stop the flow. Your conscious awareness will keep you from falling into his traps and keep the financial blessings flowing.

Now let's study the actual spiritual law of sowing and reaping to better understand how to sow and what results are promised in God's Word.

God Is Looking For Sowers to Whom He Can Give Seed

God is searching the earth for people who will receive financial seed and then sow it into good Kingdom soil. He will reward those who are obedient with abundant life. As we discussed earlier, it's important to recognize that God provides two types of seed. He gives us seed for our own use; to take care of our every need and seed to sow back into the Kingdom (tithes and gifts). As you learned in 2 Corinthians 9:10, if you use the seed properly, there is an endless supply.

Learning where to plant your seed is important as well. If you plant your financial seed in bad soil, God cannot bless it with increase, so you must learn to differentiate good soil from bad. Good ministry soil would be your church or any ministry that is legitimately doing the work of the Lord. Do your own research, before you start planting your seed into any ministry. Make sure that it is going to be used properly, so God can bless both you and the ministry.

Tithe

One way we plant seed is through the tithe. In order to completely understand the power of tithing, you must first know that everything in the world belongs to God. Psalm 24:1 says, "The earth is the Lord's, and everything in it, the world, and all who live in it." In 1 Corinthians 10:26, the apostle Paul reinforces this when he writes: "The earth is the Lord's, and everything in it." Clearly everything you have belongs to the Lord and that includes the money you earn. It all belongs to God and He just let's us use His stuff.

However, He has some expectations; the first of which is that we will give Him back the first 10% (tithe). Then He expects us to be good stewards of the other 90%; creating increase and becoming channels for His prosperity into Kingdom work here on earth.

The first recorded tithe is in Genesis 14:20, where Abraham gave 1/10th of everything to King Melchizedek, who is identified in verse 18 as a "priest of God Most High." We next see the tithe mentioned in Genesis 28:20-22, when Jacob vows, "If God will be with me and will watch over me on this journey I am taking and will give me food to eat and clothes to wear so that I return safely to my father's house, then the Lord will be my God and this stone that I have set up as a pillar will be God's house, and of all that you give me I will give you a tenth." Moses established the first law of tithing in Leviticus 27:30, "A tithe of everything from the land, whether grain from the soil or fruit from the trees, belongs to the Lord; it is holy to the Lord." This clearly shows that the tithe (which means 10%) belongs to God and is holy.

The question always comes up, as to where the tithe should be given. Must the tithe be given to a church or can it be given to a television ministry, missionary, or other good cause. Malachi 3:10 answers this very clearly, "Bring the whole tithe into the storehouse, that there may be food in my house." In the Old Testament days, the temple (church) had a storehouse. People would bring in the first fruits (tithe) of their crops and animals. The grain, fruit, and animals, would be used to first feed the priests and then to take care of the needy in that area. Obviously civilization has changed and we bring money instead of grain and animals into the storehouse. However, the place is still the same; the church and the purpose is still the same; to feed the priest (pastor, minister, rabbi) and take care of the needy. 2 Chronicles 31:4 teaches us that we give part of it to the priests so that they can devote themselves to studying the law of the Lord (Bible).

Since nearly all mention of the tithe is in the Old Testament, many people, including a few self-proclaimed Bible scholars, feel that the tithe was part of the law that was abolished by Jesus' death and resurrection. This, however, is contradicted by Jesus himself, when he acknowledges the practice of tithing in Matthew 23:23, "Woe to you, teachers of the law and Pharisees, you hypocrites! You give a tenth of your spices – mint, dill, and cumin, but you have neglected the more important matters of the law – justice, mercy, and faithfulness. You should have practiced the latter, without neglecting the former." Jesus was teaching them (and us) that first and foremost should be the laws of the Lord, but that we should also continue tithing. This clearly shows that we are supposed to be tithing 10%.

Actually, the tithe is part of God's law; the law of first things. God wants to be Lord of your life, so He wants the first fruits of the blessings He gives you. Unfortunately, many Christians make God Lord of their life, but not their wallet! Keep in mind that it's not about the money. God doesn't need your money; He walks on streets of Gold in a city with walls made from precious stones (see Revelation 21:19). He's not after your money; He's after your heart. He wants to be Lord of ALL of your life, so He wants the first 10%. If you are paying the mortgage company, bank, and credit card companies first, then you have made them Lord of your life. The first check you should write is the Lord's. Also, since all of it belongs to the Lord, you should be giving Him 10% of the gross (before taxes, 401K, health benefits, etc.) amount of your pay. If you are giving Him 10% of the net (the amount that actually shows up on your check), then you are cheating God.

The choice to tithe is always yours, as God has given each of us free will. However, Malachi 3:8 tells us how God feels about those who don't tithe. "Will a man rob God? Yet you rob me. But you ask, 'How do we rob you?' In tithes and offerings." When we don't give back to God the first 10%, we are robbing God and in verse 9 we read, "You are under a curse – the whole nation of you – because you are robbing me." So, when you choose not to tithe, you are under a curse from God. YIKES!

On the other hand, if you read Malachi 3:10-11, you will find out what happens if you do tithe. Verse 10 reads, "Bring the whole tithe into the storehouse, that there may be food in my house. 'Test me in this,' says the Lord, 'and see if I will not throw open the floodgates of heaven and pour out so much blessing that you will not have room enough for it." Here we see God's promise to reward our obedience by pouring blessings on us. Unimaginable prosperity; so much that you can't give it away fast enough!

God continues in verse 11 by showing us the other benefit of tithing, "I will prevent pests from devouring your crops, and the vines in your fields will not cast their fruit," says the Lord Almighty. What He is telling us is that if we tithe the first 10%, not only is He going to let us keep the other 90%, but He is also going to protect it from the devourer (Satan). When you tithe, you will find that this is true; the other 90% goes further than it used to. So, let's recap; if you don't tithe, you are robbing God and are under a curse. If you do tithe, God will pour out so much blessing that you don't have room enough for it and He will protect the other 90%. Sounds like a pretty easy choice, particularly when you consider that it all belongs to God anyway!

The owner of an espresso coffee shop had been attending church for years. Each Sunday he would give a few dollars in the offering, but he had never tithed. His store was constantly in a financial struggle, as was he personally. After taking this teaching on tithing to heart, he began to tithe. The very first week he tithed, his store volume doubled, as did his personal income!

Another great example is a couple who had been tithing occasionally, but not consistently and never the first check. After learning about tithing in the God's Prosperity Plan class, they began tithing. Prior to tithing, there was never enough money to make ends meet, so they didn't feel they could afford to tithe. They started writing the first check (10% of their gross income) to the church and then paid the rest of the bills. Even though their income and bills had not changed, all of a sudden there was more than enough money. God's prosperity plan does not operate under our standard rules for addition and multiplication; so don't try to figure out how that could happen, just tithe and believe.

Offerings/Gifts

Do you like receiving gifts? Of course you do. Since we are made in God's image, do you think He likes to receive gifts also? Of course He does. So many Christians think that when they are tithing, they are giving to God. This is not true and is offensive to God. The tithe belongs to God; so it cannot be a gift. Your tithe shows that you are honoring God with your obedience. Gifts, on the other hand, show your love for God. The more you give, the more you show your love for God.

The Bible gives us some hints on how we should give:

1. **Secretly** (Matthew 6:1-4), "Be careful not to do your acts of righteousness before men, to be seen by them. If you do, you will have no reward from your Father in heaven. So, when you give to the needy, do not announce it with trumpets, as the hypocrites do in the synagogues and on the streets, to be honored by men. I tell you the truth, they have received their reward in full. But when you give to the needy, do not let your left hand know what your right hand is doing, so that your giving may be in secret. Then your Father, who sees what is done in secret, will reward you." This does not mean that you can't give in a public offering; but it does mean that you shouldn't make what you are giving known to others, in order to gain the approval of man.

2. **Cheerfully** (2 Corinthians 9:7), "Each man should give what he has decided in his heart to give, not reluctantly or under compulsion, for God loves a cheerful giver." So many

Christians give out of duty or to gain God's favor, which are both wrong motives. That would be like giving a gift to a friend or family member, so they would like you better or in hopes that they would give you back a gift. God is looking for people who can get really excited about giving. When you start feeling excited about writing a big check to the church, you are ready to get blessed by God's prosperity plan.

3. **Freely** (Proverbs 11:24), "One man gives freely, yet gains even more; another withholds unduly, but comes to poverty." God's plan calls for us to give it away in order to gain even more. The more freely you give, the more freely He will give. But, don't give with that motive or you will negate the whole plan. Give freely, because God gave freely to you.

4. **Generously** (Proverbs 11:25), "A generous man will prosper; he who refreshes others will himself be refreshed." We serve a generous God; after all He gave us this big beautiful world and everything in it. Then, because we messed it up, He sent His only Son to die for our sins. Generosity is part of God's nature and part of ours. Dig past all the hardness and you will find that generous spirit. Recall what Jesus did for you and your generosity will come flowing out.

5. **Sacrificially** (Mark 12:41-44), "Jesus sat down opposite the place where the offerings were put and watched the crowd putting their money into the temple treasury. Many rich people threw in large amounts. But a poor widow came and put in two very small copper coins, worth only a fraction of a penny. Calling His disciples to Him, Jesus said, 'I tell you the truth; this poor widow has put more into the treasury than all the others. They all gave out of their wealth; but she, out of her poverty, put in everything – all she had to live on.'" Jesus was teaching the disciples (and us) that it's not about the amount, it's about the heart. The poor widow gave all she had, because she had true faith. The rich people gave

a large amount, but they had plenty more, so no need for faith. King David said that he would not give to God something that cost him nothing (2 Samuel 24:24). When you give, it should stretch your faith. If it costs you nothing, then you are not giving enough.

6. **Give Your Best** (Genesis 4:3-5), "In the course of time Cain brought some of the fruits of the soil as an offering to the Lord. But Abel brought fat portions from some of the firstborn of his flock. The Lord looked with favor on Abel and his offering, but on Cain and his offering He did not look with favor." Abel brought his first and best, while Cain brought what was left over. Too many Christians are putting their best foot forward in the world, which leaves the back foot for the Lord. Are you bringing your best to the Lord?

7. **Give from the Heart** (2 Corinthians 9:7), "Each man should give what he has decided in his heart to give . . ." The Lord will quicken to your heart with the amount He wants you to give. The Lord spoke to Abraham and told him to sacrifice his son Isaac. Abraham loved and trusted the Lord so much that he was willing to give up his only son to be obedient to the Lord. Because of Abraham's obedience, the Lord did not require the life of Isaac and He went on to bless Abraham with overwhelming financial abundance. When you sense what the Lord wants you to give, be obedient and you will be blessed abundantly in all aspects of your life.

When we give with the right motives, God's response is often to give back. Luke 6:38 says, "Give, and it will be given to you. A good measure, pressed down, shaken together and running over, will be poured into your lap. For with the measure you use, it will be measured to you." A woman who attended our God's Prosperity Plan course began to give generously, cheerfully, sacrificially, and from the heart. She was faithfully tithing and giving, even though her financial situation at times looked pretty bleak. However, God was faithful and blessed her abundantly. She owned a piece of property that she had never been able to sell. Property values had gone down and she was just hoping to recoup her initial investment. However, God had a different plan; He caused the property to sell and at a nice profit. Then she sold her home for more than she expected. The profits allowed her to pay off all her debts and now she is in an excellent financial position. She learned that if you are faithful to God, He will turn a mountain of debt into a mountain of prosperity!

A quick caution about giving and expecting a return; yes, God does promise this in His Word, but keep in mind that He is also looking at your heart. Make sure that your motives are right when you give. Also, blessings do not always come immediately and not always in the form of money. Make sure you are examining your whole life – God may be blessing you and you are not recognizing it. Be sure to thank Him for all His blessings.

Also, it's important that when you give, you do not then try to take over God's work. We reviewed 1 Corinthians 3:6 earlier, "I have planted, Apollos has watered, but God gave the increase." It's not your job to create the increase. Your only job is to plant the financial seed in good soil (your church or a good ministry). The church or ministry will water your seed and then God will cause the increase, in His time. If you are patient, God may even multiply the blessings. We see an example of this in Genesis 26:12-14, "then Isaac sowed seed in that land and received in the same year a hundred times as much as he had planted, and the Lord favored him with blessings." Jesus reinforces this in Mark 10:29-30 when He says, " 'I tell you the truth, Jesus replied, 'no one who has left home or brothers or sisters or mother or father or children or fields for me and the gospel, will fail to receive a hundred times as much in this present day and in the age to come, eternal life.'" If you are willing to be a seed sower for God, He just might bless you a hundred times over what you have given.

As we complete this section, here are a few quick warnings. It's also important that when God does open the floodgates of heaven to pour out so much blessing that you don't have room enough for it, that you are prepared for the attacks of the enemy. Once the flow of God's prosperity begins, Satan will want to try and stop the flow through spiritual attacks. Family members, friends, co-workers, and even people at your church will start to come against you. Put on the armor of God (Ephesians 6) and go to battle. Remember that it's not the people; it's the devil working through them. Also, Satan will try to throw some trials at you to make you think you are no longer in God's will. When this happens, don't start making changes; go to God and stand until you get an answer. Lastly, watch out for false prosperity. When the flow does start, don't let the devil convince you to upgrade your lifestyle by using credit. This shows a definite lack of faith and will immediately stop God's flow.

The World's Way Doesn't Work

The world's plan doesn't call for sowing and reaping. It calls for saving and hoarding. The world (Satan) wants you to believe that you will get ahead by putting money away for a rainy day. This plan may seem logical and it may even work for a while, but only God's plan will work in the long run. Proverbs 11:24-28 shows us the difference between God's plan and the world's plan, as it shows us that sowing causes increase and hoarding causes curses. God gives us seed to plant, but if it isn't planted in good soil, it can't grow. By the way, banks and the stock market are not good ground for your spiritual seed. It's ok to put some of the seed God gives you for food into a savings or investment program (more on this later). Make sure you are putting your spiritual seed (money) in God's bank (church) or invest in His securities (solid ministries) and you will enjoy benefits in both this world and the next.

God's plan calls for us to cast our seed out into the world and let God do His work. We should be casting our seed to as many of God's ministries as we can, as we never know when and how God will use our seed to create a huge harvest. Ecclesiastes 11:1-6 reads, "Cast your bread upon the waters, for after many days you will find it again. Give portions to seven, yes to eight, for you do not know what disaster may come upon the land. If clouds are full of water, they pour rain upon the earth. Whether a tree falls to the south or to the north, in the place where it falls, there will it lie. Whoever watches the wind will not plant; whoever looks at the clouds will not reap." There are no guarantees in life, except that there will be trials and tribulations. The more seed you sow, the better prepared you will be for the storms, so don't wait for the trials to come upon you, sow now.

Many Christians are saying, "When my ship comes in, then I'll give." As the scripture we just read says, "Cast your bread upon the waters; for after many days you will find it again." Only a fool looks for a ship to come in when he or she has never sent one out. If you are waiting for your ship to come in before you give, then you will be waiting a long time. You must first give and then God has something to work with; He will bring your ship in.

Asking God to give to you, before you give to Him, is like asking a wood-burning stove to produce heat without putting any wood into the stove. You must make your deposits first. Every gift you give to God is like making a deposit in your own personal faith account. God will grow your faith according to your giving. Don't try to understand how it works; just trust in the One who created the universe and you.

The world's way includes greed and coveting. The world says to pursue money and all that it can purchase, when in actuality, if you chase after money, it will run faster than you ever can. The only way you are rewarded in the world's plan is if Satan rewards you. However, if we pursue

God first, money will hunt us down and overtake us. When we are chasing after God, we can't run fast enough to outrun God's prosperity. The world's plan requires wealth in order to be happy. In God's plan, we receive our joy from the relationship with our Creator – prosperity is just an added benefit.

The world's retirement plan calls for you to invest in 401K plans, stocks, bonds, and money markets. If you have watched the news through the years, you know how unstable all of these vehicles are. If you are seeking a secure retirement plan, invest your money in God's plan – give it away now and God will give it to you later. He has promised to take care of all of our needs, if you just seek Him. Jesus taught about this in Matthew 6. He tells us not to worry about what we will wear or eat or drink, for God will take care of all these needs. 6:33 reads, "But seek first His Kingdom and His righteousness, and all these things will be given to you as well." Invest your money into God's plan and He will take care of you in your retirement. In fact, if you fully tap into God's prosperity plan, He will not only take care of all your needs, but also enable you to leave an inheritance. Proverbs 13:22 says, "A good man leaves an inheritance for his children's children, but a sinner's wealth is stored up for the righteous."

Spiritual Laws Take Precedence over Natural Laws

God existed before anything else; so spiritual laws existed before natural laws. This means that the spirit realm is actually more real than the physical realm. Unfortunately, because we can't see the spiritual realm with our physical eyes, we often think that it's not real, so we rely on natural laws. Dr. Werner Von Braun, Astrophysicist and Rocket Scientist, said, "the natural laws of the universe are so precise that we do not have any difficulty building a space ship, sending a man to the moon, and we can time the landing within the precision of a fraction of a second." He added that these natural laws are so precise that they must have been created by someone.

Here are four examples of natural laws that God created for our world:

1. **Gravity** - what goes up, must come down. A child who goes up on the roof to try to fly like Superman will quickly discover the effect of gravity.

2. **Aerodynamics** - heavy objects fly, which makes this a higher natural law than gravity. Despite the pessimism of the people around them, the Wright Brothers proved this higher natural law.

3. **Reciprocity** - what goes around comes around.

4. **Genesis** - all living things will produce after their own kind.

All the natural laws are real, but there are some higher laws. As sure as natural laws are, spiritual laws can be counted on every time. Isaiah 55:9 says, "As the heavens are higher than the earth, so are my ways higher than your ways and my thoughts than your thoughts." God's laws (spiritual laws) are higher than the natural laws. In this section, we will discuss three spiritual laws. The first is the **Law of Sin and Death** (Romans 8). This law says that the penalty for sin is death and since all mankind has sinned, each of us deserves death.

Fortunately, for all of us, God created the second, higher spiritual law; the **Law of Spirit of Life in Jesus Christ** (Also in Romans 8). This law says that if any man (or woman) is in Christ, his sin debt has been paid for and he is righteous in God's eyes.

The third spiritual law is the **Law of Sowing and Reaping**. This law says that what ever you plant and tend, will reproduce. Ralph Waldo Emerson called this the "law of laws." God calls us to give in order to live and live in order to give. Our life's harvest is dependent solely on what we sow now.

God's Plan Works with the Spiritual Laws

When you enter into God's prosperity plan, you are operating within the powerful spiritual laws of Spirit of Life and Sowing & Reaping. As you learned in Chapter 2, the first qualification for entering God's plan is to be a born-again believer. This means that you are obeying the law of Spirit of Life. Then, as you begin to give (based on what you have learned in the last two chapters), you begin to benefit from the law of Sowing and Reaping. Paul understood the power of the law of sowing and reaping, when he said, "Remember this: Whoever sows sparingly will also reap sparingly, and whoever sows generously will also reap generously." Paul knew that God was his source and that the more we give to God the more He gives back to us. In its simplicity, that is the law of sowing and reaping.

Giving is critical to God's plan, but so is receiving. Have you ever seen a father come home after a business trip and the kids all run up and stretch their arms up to daddy? That's what God is looking for. He's looking for that child-like nature in us. Earlier in the book we established that God's prosperity plan is part of the Kingdom of God (or of Heaven). Jesus taught, "I tell you the truth, unless you change and become like little children, you will never enter the kingdom of heaven." We must learn to take up the receiving posture of a child, giving love to the Father and raising open arms to receive.

One of the unique aspects of God's plan is that it doesn't work with the standard mathematical system of addition and multiplication. It is not bound by natural laws or by the world's economy. As when you plant a single apple seed you don't just get one apple, you get a tree with many apples; it's the same when you sow into God's prosperity plan.

In the world's plan there is always lack; as there will always be the rich and the poor. In God's plan, there is never lack. When you make the commitment to be a part of God's plan, God gives you special grace, so that you will never be in lack. Paul discusses this in 2 Corinthians 9:8, "And God is able to make all grace abound to you, so that in all things at all times, having all that you need, you will abound in every good work." In His plan, God provides every thing that we need, so we will not need things from the world.

The law of sowing and reaping is a most powerful law. It offers us the opportunity to have everything we want in life and to lay up treasures in heaven, so that we can enjoy both earthly and eternal lives. God truly wants to bless His children and has established the sowing and reaping system, so that we might receive the prosperity He has intended. Make sure you fully grasp the power of this law. First, sow prosperity into your heart by memorizing and internalizing the promises of God. Then begin to sow the financial seeds that God has given you into good ground through your tithes and offerings. Then be patient and wait for God to bring a bountiful harvest.

Chapter Four Discussion Questions

1. How does sowing into the flesh hinder God's prosperity plan in your life?

2. Why is prayer an important part of God's plan? Discuss your prayer life?

3. What are the benefits of planting God's Word in the garden of your heart?

4. Discuss your plan for increasing your daily time in the Bible.

5. Why is it important to weed the garden of your heart every day?

6. How does God expect you to handle the seed He gives you?

7. Discuss the five hindrances mentioned in this chapter and how you can avoid them.

8. Discuss what the tithe is and why it is important to God's plan.

9. Discuss a giving plan that includes the tithe and a giving program.

10. What are the seven things the Bible teaches about giving? Discuss each.

11. What is the Law of Sowing and Reaping? Discuss.

Five

Partnership Has
Its Privileges

Chapter 5

Partnership Has Its Privileges

Partnership is a powerful concept that was developed by God. Although worldly people have probably enjoyed greater benefit from partnership; Christians are finally catching on. In John Maxwell's book, <u>The Power of Partnership in the Church</u>, he tells the story of an ice cream vendor, Arnold Fornachou, at the 1904 world's fair, who ran out of bowls in the middle of the fair. In the booth next door was Ernest Hamwi, a pastry chef who was offering a wafer-thin Perisian pastry called zalabia. While Arnold's booth was swamped with people, no one was buying from Ernest. When Ernest saw that Arnold was in trouble, he quickly shaped his warm zalabia into a cone shape, put a scoop of ice cream into it and offered this unique combination to a customer. It was an instant hit and became know as World's Fair Cornucopias. This powerful partnership resulted in what we now know as ice cream cones. Ecclesiastes 4:9 reads, "Two are better than one, because they have a good return for their work." Arnold and Ernest proved this in 1904 and it's been proven many, many times since.

Partnership with man can be very powerful, but partnership with God is the most important partnership. In this chapter, you will learn about partnerships, how to partner with God, and what happens to your life when you do. You will also learn how to join with God and man to form amazing prosperity partnerships.

First, it would be a good idea to define partnership. The American Heritage Dictionary defines partnership as, "A relationship between individuals or groups that is characterized by mutual cooperation and responsibility, as for the achievement of a specified goal." God partnered with man right from the beginning. He didn't just create the earth and then rule it himself. He decided to share it with man and in fact turned dominion of the planet over to man. God partnered with Moses to bring the Israelites out of slavery. He partnered with Mary to give birth to His own Son, Jesus. Then He partnered with Jesus to bridge the gap between our sin and God's holiness. God has been partnering with man ever since and He wants to partner with you.

According to John Maxwell, in his book <u>The Power of Partnership in the Church</u>, partnership is not something that just happens; there are four stages:

1. **Friendship** – this is the stage where you get to know the person and create a relationship. Very often the beginnings of intimacy will form during this stage. Chemistry is very important during this first stage in order for the partners to want to move on to stage two.

2. **Formation** – during this stage unique talents and abilities of the partners are identified. The part each will play in the partnership is determined, so that each can contribute equally.

3. **Functioning** – next the partners begin working together in cooperation. If the partnership is sound, there will be unity and things will run smoothly.

4. **Fruitfulness** – this is the stage where creativity and innovation begins to abound. Results are excellent; goals are being met.

If you are married or have had a business partnership, you probably recognized these steps in your human partnership. Partnership with God goes through the same stages:

1. **Friendship** – during this stage you are convicted by God to make changes in your life and are lead to accept Christ as your Lord and Savior. You begin reading the Bible and gaining greater understanding of God's character. Slowly, as

you get to know God, you begin to develop a relationship with Him.

2. **Formation** – the more you study the Bible, the more you understand your position as an adopted child of God; a co-heir with Jesus. Your life begins to change as you release yourself to God's life-changing touch. You begin to exhibit the fruit of the spirit (refer to Galatians 5:22). God will also begin to reveal the spiritual gifts He has given you to accomplish your purpose here on earth. It is during this stage, you will begin to understand your part in God's grand plan.

3. **Functioning** – now that you understand your spiritual gifts, God will likely lead you to some form of ministry work, so that you can utilize your gifts. As you partner with a ministry and with God, you will begin to experience a feeling of cooperation with God.

4. **Fruitfulness** – during this stage you will notice a higher level of creativity and innovation, as God begins to release the creative part of you. Part of God's character is creativity. Since we are made in God's image (Genesis 1:26), creativity is part of our character as well. During this stage you will start to see results, such as people getting saved and turning their lives around.

Partnerships are clearly beneficial to your financial situation as well. Here are some of the benefits of partnering with God:

1. **Earn More** – If you have been struggling financially, this is going to be great news. If you partner with God and His anointed ministries, you will earn more. This is a promise, right from the Word of God. Look at Ecclesiastes 4:9, "Two are better than one, because they have a good return for their work." In Mark 10:29-30, Jesus says, "No one who has left home or brothers or sisters or mother or father or children or fields for me and the gospel will fail to receive a <u>hundred times</u> as much in this present age and in

the age to come, eternal life." Jesus is telling us that if we are willing to give up the things of the world to partner with Him, He will prosper us in both this world and the next.

2. **Multiplies Your Potential** – Geese are interesting creatures. Have you ever noticed that they always fly in a "V". Even if there are just two geese, one will fly in front and the other behind and off to the side. A flock of geese adds at least 70% to its flying range by flying in the "V" formation. One goose will take the lead position and the others will fall in behind. When the lead goose gets tired, he will fall to the back and another will take its place. This formation allows the geese behind to draft off the goose in front, thus making it less strenuous. If a goose is sick or injured, two other geese will drop out with it until it is either gets well or dies. They will then join another formation, in order to catch up with their flock. Another interesting fact is that the geese behind the leader will honk encouragement to the leader and those in front. This is an example of true partnership – and teamwork. TEAM means Together Everyone Accomplishes More. Jesus recognized this principle, as He chose a team to change the world. When you team up with God and God's ministries, you multiply your potential.

3. **Recover Quicker from Trouble** – Ecclesiastes 4:10 says, "If one falls down, his friend can help him up. But pity the man who falls and has no one to help him up!" God did not mean for us to be alone. First, by partnering with God, you are never alone. When the financial troubles (or any other type) come, God is always there to give you wisdom and guide you. Second, God means for us to partner with other Christians. We are to have prayer and accountability partners and spiritual mentors. Joshua partnered with Moses, Aaron, and Hur to win the battle against the Amalekites. Jesus sent the disciples out in twos, so that they could support each other. Paul mentored Timothy, so he could accomplish the plan that God had for him. You should have a prayer partner, who is well aware of your financial

situation and goals and is praying for you daily. You should also have a spiritual mentor who is also aware of your financial situation and goals; who can give you spiritual counsel and also pray for you. Partnership with God and other believers will help you stay away from trouble and recover quickly when it does enter your life.

4. **Dream Bigger** – When you partner with God, you get to dream His dreams for your life. Is there any question that He has bigger dreams for you than you have for yourself? Just before Jesus ascended into heaven, He said, "I tell you the truth, anyone who has faith in me will do what I have been doing. He will do even greater things than these, because I am going to the Father." This is a pretty amazing statement, considering all that Jesus did in three short years on earth. It's because He recognized that if we partnered with the Father, He would send us the Holy Spirit and we would receive the associated power. God has much bigger expectations for our lives than what we have, so when you begin to dream big dreams, know that they are from God and that if you just start walking down that path of obedience, He will help you accomplish these dreams.

5. **Able to Resist the Devil Better** – The devil is like a wolf; he likes to separate a lone sheep from the flock and devour him or her. When we partner with God and with other believers, it's much harder for Satan to attack us. Ecclesiastes 4:12 reads, "Though one may be overpowered, two can defend themselves. A cord of three strands is not quickly broken." There are several key concepts in this scripture. First, as we know from the world, it is much harder for a mugger to attack two people who are walking along together, than an individual. In the spiritual realm, it is much more difficult for the devil to attack two Christians who are in unity, in Christ. Partner with God and another believer or ministry, and you are like the three strand cord mentioned in Ecclesiastes 4:12.

Three Partners in Ministry

In ministry there are three partners. We see these partners illustrated in 1 Corinthians 3:6 (NIV) where the apostle Paul says, "I planted the seed, Apollos watered it, but God made it grow." The three partners in ministry are you, the church/ministry, and God. Here are the parts each play:

You – Your part is to seek God's guidance in finding good ground (church or ministry) and then plant your financial seed through tithes and offerings.

Church or Ministry –The church or ministry not only provides good ground for the seeds, but also waters and cultivates your seed.

God – As the scripture says, God makes it grow or as the King James translation says, "God gave the increase." He creates the increase and not in the way we are used to in the world. Quite often God will multiply the harvest. Matthew 13:8 says, "Still other seed fell on good soil, where it produced a crop – a hundred, sixty or thirty times what was sown." This scripture is part of the Parable of the Sower and is primarily referring to the Word of God as seed, but it also has a second financial meaning. When you plant the seed that God has given you to plant, into good ground, it is quite possible that you will receive a hundred, sixty, or thirty-fold return. That's a lot better return than 6% in a money market, wouldn't you say?

There have been many students in the God's Prosperity Plan class who have reported giving a gift to the church or a solid ministry, only to have God return it multiplied in the form of an unexpected gift. Recently, Karen and I (Rod) felt God telling us to give a gift worth $200 to a young couple in our church. We didn't really have $200 available, but were obedient. The next day we received an unexpected check for just under $300! We planted the seed in good ground and God produced the increase.

God Prospers His Partners

The Bible is very clear about what God's intentions and promises are; when you partner with God and do it His way, He will prosper you. Psalm 1:1-3 reads, "Blessed is the man who does not walk in the counsel of the wicked or stand in the way of sinners or sit in the seat of mockers. But his delight is in the law of the Lord, and on his law he meditates day and night. He is like a tree planted by streams of water, which yields its fruit in season and whose leaf does not wither. Whatever he does prospers." In this scripture we see that if you stop doing things the worldly way and walk with God by reading and meditating on the scriptures in the Bible every day, then He will prosper you. You notice that it doesn't say that God may prosper you or could prosper you; it says that He WILL prosper you. This is a promise from God, the one who created everything and since God cannot lie, we know that He will fulfill His side of this promise. If we want God to prosper us, then all we need to do is do our part of what Psalm 1:1-3 says.

2 Chronicles 26:5 says, "He continued to seek God in the days of Zechariah, who had understanding through the vision of God and as long as he sought the Lord, God prospered him." This scripture references Uzziah, who at age sixteen was made king. This clearly was a blessing from God and as the scripture reads, as long as he sought the Lord, he prospered. God is the same today, as He was then. If you seek the Lord and partner with Him, He will prosper you.

Once again, in Deuteronomy 29:9 we see that if we do things God's way, He will prosper us. "Carefully follow the terms of this covenant, so that you may prosper in everything you do." God wants to be Lord of your life and rightly so. All you have to do is let Him take His rightful place in your life and then follow Him. If there is anyone in your life who could take you to unbelievable prosperity, it's God.

Ok, we've examined several scriptures that clearly show us what we need to do in order for God to prosper us, which is to partner with Him. The Bible highlights several people who partnered with God and prospered. The first is Abram (later Abraham). In Genesis 12:1-3 we read, "The Lord had said to Abram, 'Leave your country, your people and your father's household and go to the land I will show you. I will make you into a great nation and I will bless you; I will make your name great, and you will be a blessing. I will bless those who bless you, and whoever curses you I will curse; and all peoples on earth will be blessed through you.'" As we can see, sometimes when we partner with God, He will ask us to give up the things of the world. He asked Abram to leave everything he had and knew, in order to make God the Lord of his life. He did and was prospered, as we see in Genesis 13:2, "Abram had become very wealthy in livestock and in silver and gold." If you choose to partner with God, He may ask you to give up the things of the world and follow Him. If you choose to obey, He will prosper you!

The second example is King David. In 1 Samuel 16:13, we see God anoint a young shepherd boy named David to be the next king. If God can create a great king from a lowly shepherd boy, imagine what He could do with you. The key once again was partnership and obedience. David was willing to partner with God and believe in Him, so the Lord prospered him. We see the evidence of David's prosperity in 1 Chronicles 29:28, "He died at a good old age, having enjoyed long life, wealth, and honor. His son Solomon succeeded him as king."

The last example is David's son Solomon. In 1 Kings 3:5 we see the partnership emerge, "At Gibeon the Lord appeared to Solomon during the night in a dream, and God said, 'Ask for whatever you want me to give you.'" WOW, wouldn't that be awesome; to have God show up in a dream and ask what you want? What would you ask for? Well, Solomon was very smart; he asked for wisdom (1 Kings 3:9). Because Solomon was willing to partner with God, He not only gave Solomon wisdom, but also health, long life, and great wealth.   Solomon partnered with God and he prospered.

God wants you to be another great example. He wants you to partner with Him and be obedient to His plans to prosper you (Jeremiah 29:11). Cast aside the world's prosperity plan and follow God into divine prosperity.

Keys to Partnership with God

The Bible clearly outlines the keys to partnering with God:

1. **See where God is working** – Ask God to open the eyes of your spirit to be able to see where He is working in your world. Sometimes we are so blind to what He is doing that we miss opportunities to partner with God. Jesus recognized this in John 4:35, when He said, "Do you not say, 'Four months more and then the harvest? I tell you open your eyes and look at the fields! They are ripe for harvest.'" He saw that the people were blind to the harvest. Today, we believers are still blind to the harvest – both in terms of souls and finances. The key here is prayer. The more time you spend in prayer, the more your spiritual eyes will be opened.

2. **Listening for God's still small voice** – God is talking to us all the time. The problem is that we don't hear His voice over the noise of our world. Set aside some quiet time each day for meditation over the Word and prayer. Ask God what part He wants you to play today. If you study Ezekiel 2, starting in verse 1, you will see a pattern for how God partners with His chosen people. First, He speaks to you (verse 1). Then the Holy Spirit comes upon you (verse 2), which opens your spiritual eyes and ears. Next, He gives you an assignment (verse 3), which you will be able to carry out because the Holy Spirit is with you. The key is to hear His voice, so you can receive the Spirit and assignment. Otherwise, He will pass you up and find someone else to do the job.

3. **Be obedient** – In Genesis 12:1, when God told Abram to leave his country, people, and Father, Abram obeyed and was blessed abundantly. On the flipside, a rich young man asked Jesus what he needed to do to have eternal life. Jesus told him to obey all the commandments and to sell everything he owned, give the proceeds to the poor, and follow Him. This young man did not understand the power of obedience and he passed up the opportunity to follow Jesus. He chose earthly wealth over spiritual wealth. It is quite possible that if the young man had been obedient, that Jesus just might have restored his wealth and added to it a hundred fold. We will never know, but if you are asked to give up what you have to follow Jesus, confirm that it is God and if so, do it!

4. **Let God strengthen You** – God loves to stretch us out of our comfort zones, so He will likely ask you to do things that are not within your gifting. He does this so that we learn to lean on Him, instead of our own abilities. Each time God takes you out of your comfort zone, He will build you up so that you can handle it. Commit yourself to the Lord and He will strengthen you. 2 Chronicles 16:9 says, "For the eyes of the Lord range throughout the earth to strengthen those whose hearts are fully committed to Him." Isaiah 41:10 reads, "So do not fear, for I am with you; do not be dismayed, for I am your God. I will strengthen you and help you; I will uphold you with my righteous right hand. 2nd Thessalonians 3:3, says, "But the Lord is faithful and He will strengthen and protect you from the evil one." If you are obedient, God will strengthen you, so that you can accomplish the work that will lead to your prosperity.

5. **Don't limit God** – God has big plans for you. Don't let your limited dreams and plans block God's plan for you. Most likely, when you were young you had great dreams that God had given you. Now, if you are like most people, your dreams have been crushed by life. God wants to rekindle those dreams. Also, keep in mind that our dreams are always

so much smaller than His dreams for us. Let Him do the dreaming and see where He takes you.

A great example of this is the story of a young man whose lifelong dream had been to be a missionary. It looked like everything was going to work out, until his wife took ill and they realized that she would not be able to handle the rigorous missionary life. Crushed, he went to work for his father who owned a small business that produced unfermented wine for church communion services. His father grew older and soon the young man took over operation of the business. One day, he realized that he could still have an impact on the world for Christ. He worked hard and built the company into a large business. His last name was Welch and today his grape juice is sold around the world and he has used his wealth to fund hundreds of missionaries. He had a plan, but God had a bigger plan. Get excited about the big plan God has for you.

6. **Giving and receiving** – Give yourself fully to God. Give Him your time, talents, energy, and money. A partnership is all about giving and receiving. You give and God receives. Then God gives and you receive. He loves to partner with people who will become channels for the Kingdom. People who will give and receive, over and over again.

The first step is for you to give. Then you need to prepare yourself to receive, because He wants to pour prosperity into your life. Remember God's promise in Malachi 3:10, "'Bring the whole tithe into the storehouse, that there may be food in my house. Test me in this,' says the Lord Almighty, 'and see if I will not throw open the floodgates of heaven and pour out so much blessing that you will not have room enough for it.'" Are you ready to receive that huge of a blessing?

Keys to God-Based Human Partnerships

Since many of your partnerships are going to be with people, in this section you will learn how to create God-based partnerships. Here are six keys:

1. **Partner with godly people**. Paul addressed this issue with the Corinthians in 2 Corinthians 6:14-17 "Do not be yoked together with unbelievers. For what do righteousness and wickedness have in common? Or what fellowship can light have with darkness? What harmony is there between Christ and Belial (devil or Satan)? What does a believer have in common with an unbeliever? What agreement is there between the temple of God and idols? For we are the temple of the living God. As God has said: 'I will live with them and walk among them and I will be their God, and they will be my people. Therefore come out from them and be separate,' says the Lord. 'Touch no unclean thing, and I will receive you.'"

In 2 Chronicles 18 through 20 we see King Jehoshaphat partnering with an ungodly person. The result was ruin and death. Bad partnerships can affect your marriage, business, job and ministry. Establish your values and then only partner with people who have the same values. Stand up for your values, because if you stand for nothing, you will fall for anything.

2. **Partner with people who have the same vision and goals**. Goals and vision, of course, should be within God's will and purpose for your life. You can't partner effectively with someone who is going in a different direction. Have you ever been in a 3-legged race? What happens if you both try to go a different direction? The same thing happens in partnerships. Before you partner with someone, communicate your vision and goals. Make sure you have a good match and then invest some time in prayer to make sure that this is a partnership of which God approves.

3. **Partner with people you like and can work or live with**. Jesus didn't choose the religious leaders of His time to partner with, because He knew that they wouldn't cooperate with His Father's plan. Whether you are partnering with someone for marriage, ministry, or business, make sure this is someone you like and would enjoy spending time with. The spirit of strife within a partnership can stop the flow of blessings quicker than any other demonic spirit.

4. **Partner with people who are as committed as you are**. Great partnerships require commitment. Look at Jesus and the disciples. They were all committed. Find partners who are committed to do God's will. Look what Jesus said in Luke 9:23, "Then He said to them all: 'If anyone would come after me, he must deny himself and take up his cross daily and follow me.'" This is the kind of commitment God expects of us and we should expect of others. Part of commitment is also submission. We must all be willing to fully submit to God's will in our life and our partnerships. Submission shows that we have given up control to God and His plan. This is a huge key to God's prosperity plan.

5. **Partner with people who are complimentary**. No, not people who compliment you all the time; rather those who have complimentary gifts and personality. 1st Corinthians 12:4 says, "There are different kinds of gifts, but the same Spirit." Verse 7 says, "Now to each one manifestations of the Spirit is given for common good." In 1 Corinthians 12:12, Paul talks about the body parts working together in flawless cooperation. Imagine if your eyes didn't work with your brain or your feet went a different direction than your head. Your life would be chaos. It's the same in the body of Christ. We must all work together in flawless cooperation for the good of the whole body. Each using his or her gifts to further the Kingdom. By doing this, we will all benefit and receive God's blessings.

6. **Partner with God's anointed leaders**. God places His anointing on certain people and when we partner with those

people, we share in that anointing. In Exodus 17, we see Joshua partner with Moses, God's anointed leader. When Moses held his arms in the air, Joshua won battles, but when Moses would drop his arms, Joshua's army would be routed. When Moses got tired, Aaron and Hur jumped in and partnered with Moses to hold up his arms and Joshua was victorious. Partner with anointed leaders through giving and prayer and you will receive God's blessing.

Prosperity Partnerships

There are prosperity partnerships available in all parts of your life. Here is a quick review:

1. **God** – This is the first and most important of the prosperity partnerships. God wants His kids to partner with Him in all aspects of life. If we do, He will prosper us. After all, this is God's prosperity plan.

2. **Spouse/Family** – Your spouse (if you are married) and family are also important prosperity partners. Next to God they are your most important partners. Make sure that you are always in unity with them. Also, solicit their ongoing support and prayer coverage.

3. **Church/Ministry** – This is where you will plant your seeds, so make sure that you check to be sure that it's good ground. You may also find people who can provide you with prayer coverage, spiritual guidance and counsel, when needed.

4. **Business/Job** – Your business or job is not your source; God is. However, God very often will use your business or job to prosper you. It is also a good idea to watch for open doors in the form of career changes, home businesses, and investment opportunities. Make sure that you confirm these with God through prayer and fasting. Do not make big changes until you have received a clear confirmation. You may also want to get spiritual counsel when making big decisions. Proverbs 11:14 says, "Where there is no counsel,

the people fail; But in the multitude of counselors, there is safety."

Partnerships Are Contagious

God created us for partnership. We are most comfortable and happy when we are in partnerships. You will also find that when you partner with others, it will spawn other partnerships. We see evidence of this in the New Testament, as Jesus partnered with the twelve disciples. When He ascended into heaven, He left the salvation of the entire world in the hands of a motley group of men.

So the story goes, Jesus ascended into heaven and the archangel Michael asked Him how things went. Jesus said that all went exactly as planned and that He left the salvation of the entire world in the hands of eleven men. Michael gasped and said, "Eleven humans? What's plan B?" To which Jesus replied, "There is no plan B."

Jesus was there in the beginning when God created partnerships. He then modeled partnership while He walked the earth and the disciples went on to create similar partnerships. Today we see millions of partnerships that make up what we call Christianity.

Another great story of partnership comes from John Maxwell's book, The Power of Partnership in Church. This story is titled "One Partnership Produces More Partnerships." Angus McGillivray was a Scottish prisoner in a prison camp filled with American, Australian, and British soldiers – the same soldiers who built the famous Bridge over the River Kwai. During Angus' time there the camp atmosphere had become almost hostile as prisoners stole from each other daily to survive.

To protect their belongings, the Scottish prisoners developed a buddy system. Every Scot had a partner know as their "mucker." Angus was given a mucker who was nearing death. In fact, everyone else had given up on him. But Angus did all he could to keep his mucker alive, from

100

surrendering his own blanket to skipping meals each day. Miraculously, his mucker regained health. But shortly thereafter, Angus grew weak and died – a result of starvation and exhaustion.

Word spread about Angus' death and prisoners were moved. They decided to pool their talents for the betterment of the entire camp. One prisoner made violins, another was a carpenter, another was a skilled musician, and another a professor. Soon the camp had developed an entire orchestra of hand-made instruments and began what they called "The Church without Walls." The services were so compelling, even the Japanese guards attended. Amazingly, in the weeks to come the prisoners also went on to start a university, a library, and a hospital . . . all the result of one partnership. When one partnership leads the way, others will follow.

When we accept Christ into our lives, the Bible tells us that we become co-heirs with Jesus (Romans 8:17). This means we are to be partners with Jesus for His work here on earth. As a co-heir, we have inherited everything that the Father gave to the Son (which was everything). All we have to do is agree to partner with Him. How do we do this? Look around and see where God is working, then ask to partner with Him. God is talking to us all the time; listen carefully and obey. Let Him take you out of your comfort zones and into His comfort zones. Give yourself freely to this divine partnership and plan, and then get ready to receive His immense blessings.

God wants to partner with you. It's part of His prosperity plan to do so. When you partner with God and the ministries that He has anointed, you create that three strand cord referenced earlier. Ecclesiastes 4:12 says, "a cord of three strands is not quickly broken." When you are operating on your own, it's easy for Satan and his demons to distract you and foil your plans, but when you form Holy partnerships, Satan can't touch them.

God has been partnering with man, to accomplish things, since the beginning of our time here on earth. In the rest of this chapter, you will learn about God's Promises, Power, and Privileges, when we partner with Him.

God's Promises to His Partners

The world is touting its prosperity plan on television, in magazines, in books, and on the Internet. Satan has managed to infiltrate all of the media with his wealth-building message. Don't be deceived; God has a much better plan! In this section, you will learn more about His promises.

Paul addresses the first promise in Philippians 1:2-11, "Grace and peace to you from God our Father and the Lord Jesus Christ. I thank my God every time I remember you. In all my prayers for all of you, I always pray with joy because of your partnership in the gospel from the first day until now, being confident of this, that He who began a good work in you will carry it on to completion until the day of Christ Jesus. It is right for me to feel this way about all of you, since I have you in my heart, for whether I am in chains or defending and confirming the gospel, all of you share in God's grace with me. God can testify how I long for all of you with the affection of Christ Jesus. And this is my prayer: that your love may abound more and more in knowledge and depth of insight, so that you may be able to discern what is best and may be pure and blameless until the day of Christ, filled with the fruit of righteousness that comes through Jesus Christ – to the glory and praise of God." Paul recognized and was sharing with the Philippians that when we partner with God, we share in God's grace. When we examine the Greek word that is translated as grace, we see that one of the definitions is "favor". God is promising that if we partner fully with Him, we share in His favor!

You will find the second promise in Philippians 4:19, where Paul says, "And my God will meet all your needs according to His glorious riches in Christ Jesus." How vast are God's riches? Well, since we know that everything belongs to Him, His riches would be beyond our comprehension. His promise is that if we partner fully with Him, He will meet ALL our needs according to His riches, not ours. Isn't that exciting? No matter what your current financial circumstances, God has more than enough to totally turn it around.

The third promise can be found in Luke 6:38, where Jesus teaches, "Give, and it will be given to you. A good measure, pressed down, shaken together and running over, will be poured into your lap. For with the measure you use, it will be measured to you." This promise is very clear, if you partner with God by giving, He will give back in a greater measure. In fact, He wants to give back to us abundantly greater than what we give. When a child gives a very simple gift to a loving parent, the parent wants to give so much more back to the child. God is no different; He loves to heap gifts on His kids when they partner with Him by giving to support His many ministries here on earth.

God's Power to His Partners

The world's prosperity plan is very individualistic. It is focused on "me and no more." Individualism is the devil's scheme. He wants to keep us alone and focused on ourselves, instead of God and our fellow man. The devil really doesn't want us to succeed. The Bible says that he came to "steal, kill, and destroy" mankind. One way he does that is by sucking us into the world's prosperity system, which always leads to destruction. It keeps us away from a relationship with God and quite often results in bankruptcies, divorces, and suicides.

God's plan is based on partnership with Him and others. His plan results in synergy, which always produces better results. Think about a horse-drawn cart. One horse can pull a certain size load at a certain speed. Two horses can pull a load more than twice as large and pull it more than twice as fast. Partnership increases the power.

When we fully engage God's prosperity plan, He gives us power that is not available in the world's plan. For example, the world's plan is based on simple addition and multiplication. It is very predictable. Whereas, God has His own multiplication plan that just doesn't fit our financial paradigm. Since Jesus used farming a lot in His parables, a farming example would be very appropriate here. When you sow a single corn seed, what do you get? If this were the world's plan, you would get one corn kernel in return. In God's plan you get a stalk with a number of ears of corn, with many kernels on each ear. If you plant a single apple seed, do you get one apple or a tree full of apples that grow every year for the life of the tree? The old saying goes, "you can count the seeds in an apple, but you can't count the apples in a seed." God has a much more powerful system than the devil's system. The Bible tells us that He who is in us (the Holy Spirit) is greater than he who is in the world (the devil).

When we partner with God He let's us enter into His Kingdom and His Power. He allows us to leave the earthly addition system which results in $2 + 2 = 4$. We have the privilege of participating in the law of sowing and reaping, which was discussed in the last chapter. This is God's version of multiplication and it does not resemble the world's system at all.

As we discussed earlier in the book, when we sow a seed into the ground, we don't get one seed back; we get a whole crop. One corn kernel will result in many ears of corn and hundreds of kernels. One apple seed grows an entire tree that will produce a crop of apples year after year. When one person accepts Christ into his or her heart, a disciple is born, but one disciple planted firmly in the Kingdom results in many other lives impacted and many new disciples of Christ.

The world operates based on the law of Economics which says that a certain amount of effort with result in a relational return. It also operates based on supply and demand. As long as there is a demand, there will be a supply.

God's system isn't controlled by any of these worldly laws. It operates with a whole different paradigm. We see examples of this in the Bible, when Jesus feeds 5000+ people with a two fish and five loaves of bread (Mark 6:30-44). How was this possible? It wasn't in the worldly system of economics, but completely possible in God's system. The really interesting thing is that after everyone ate, there were twelve baskets of pieces left. God has more than enough for every situation. Jesus understood that if He made a demand on the unlimited supply of His Father, God would provide more than what was needed. Are you making a demand on God's unlimited supply by first giving your tithes and offerings consistently and then asking God for prosperity?

God's Privilege to His Partners

When you partner with God, you become a privileged member of His family. He gives you special access to His knowledge and wisdom. As more Christians enter God's prosperity plan, more of His wisdom and knowledge will flow through the earth. Habakkuk 2:14 reads, "For the earth will be filled with the knowledge of the glory of the Lord, as the waters cover the sea." In other words, we will be swimming (or drowning, in some cases) in the glorious knowledge of the Lord, which of course will include knowledge about finances.

In these end times, the Lord is going to make a wealth transfer. He has allowed the wicked to obtain massive wealth by using the devil's prosperity plan. However, as it says in Proverbs 13:22, "But the wealth of the sinner is stored up for the righteous." God is already working in this area. He is beginning the transfer to the righteous who are operating in His prosperity plan. Soon, God will begin to pour out prosperity on His children unlike anything that has been seen throughout history. By working within God's plan, you will be in a receiving mode for this amazing wealth transfer.

The most exciting part is that since you were compelled to read this book and are already beginning to make changes in your financial life, you are among those God chose before the beginning of time to receive His flow of prosperity. He knew that you had what it takes to become a channel for His riches. We see a great example of this in 1st Kings 17, when during a great drought, the prophet Elijah approaches a widow and asks her for a cup of water and a bread cake. She tells him that she only has enough for a cake for herself and her son and then they would die. Elijah tells the widow to make a cake for him first and then make cakes for her and her son. She is obedient and her flour and oil did not run out until the drought was over. The widow understood how to enter the flow of God's prosperity – by giving to God's anointed people. She gave sacrificially, because she had faith in God. Are you giving in that same way? If so, you too will be blessed by entering God's prosperity flow. If you are not, then change your ways quickly and enter the flow of His blessing.

So many people would love to partner with the likes of Bill Gates, but partnering with God is the greatest privilege on the earth today. There is no one richer or more powerful than God, so what are you waiting for, begin partnering with Him today and join the privileged few.

1. Read Ecclesiastes 4:9 and discuss why two working together produce better results.

2. What are the four stages of partnership? Discuss where you are with God.

3. What are the five benefits of partnering with God? Discuss how you have benefited.

4. Who are the three partners in God's prosperity plan and what parts do they play?

5. What did God ask of Abram before prospering him? What is He asking of you?

6. David was willing to partner with God, discuss your willingness.

7. What are the six keys to partnership with God? Discuss each.

8. What are the six keys to God-based human partnerships? Discuss each.

9. What are the four prosperity partnerships? Discuss each.

10. How are partnerships contagious? Give some examples from your own life.

11. How does the three strand cord in Ecclesiastes 4:12 work?

12. What are some of the prosperity promises God has made in the Bible? Discuss each.

13. What power do we receive when we partner with God?

14. What are the privileges of partnering with God?

Six

Learning to Be
A Good Steward

Chapter 6

Learning to Be a Good Steward

As you learned in the last chapter, God's prosperity plan requires partnership. God supplies all the stuff and we manage it. 1 Corinthians 10:26 reads, "The earth is the Lord's, and everything in it." Everything belongs to God, even those things you refer to as your own – your house, car, clothes, boat, motor home, computer, and money. God has loaned you all His stuff and expects you to be a good steward.

Definition of Steward

What is a steward? The dictionary defines a steward as "somebody who manages the property, finances, or household of another." The general definition you will find in the church is "a guardian of the affairs of God." The definition we are going to use in this chapter is a compilation of both (with a little extra): "Someone who manages the resources God gives him/her in such a way as to cause increase."

Areas of Stewardship

According to the Bible, we are to be good stewards in three areas: (1) Manifold grace of God; (2) Mysteries of God; (3) God's household. The Bible is very explicit about our stewardship in these three areas. In the following sections we will examine each of these areas.

Manifold Grace of God

1 Peter 4:10 reads, "As each one has received a gift, minister it to one another, as good stewards of the manifold

grace of God." God gives each of us certain gifts that are to be used to minister the grace of God to people who don't know Him and also those who do. It is God's grace alone that saves us and insures our place in heaven. It is also God's grace alone that enables us to participate in His prosperity plan. There is no one on this planet that is good enough to get into either God's prosperity plan for this earth or His eternal plan in heaven. As was discussed back in Chapter 2 (Qualifications for Divine Prosperity), the first qualification is that you must be born again; meaning that you have repented of your sins and have turned your life over to Christ as your Lord and Savior. So, by His grace you are saved. Then you are to use what God has given you to administer the message of God's grace to others. It's all part of His grand plan.

God has grace for the murderer, child molester, spouse abuser, thief, terrorist, adulterer, liar, gossip, slanderer and all others who have sinned at least one time in their life. It is an important part of our job as a steward, to explain this grace to others. So many people think that they must work hard to get in God's good graces. They must pray certain prayers, attend certain services, worship on certain days, read the Bible a certain amount, and perform certain acts that would make them holy to God. All of these things have been created by man, in hopes that they will draw him closer to God. The reality is that God has made it very simple. He sent His Son Jesus to earth to die as a legal atonement for our sins. His part was hard; our part is easy. Romans 10:9-11 makes our part very clear, "That if you confess with your mouth, 'Jesus is Lord,' and believe in your heart that God raised him from the dead, you will be saved. For it is with your heart that you believe and are justified, and it is with your mouth that you confess and are saved." Verse 13 sums it all up, "Everyone who calls on the name of the Lord will be saved."

So, the first area in which we are to be good stewards is the Grace of God. As believers in Christ, it is our obligation to share the good news with others.

Mysteries of God

1 Corinthians 4:1 reads, "Let a man so consider us, as servants of Christ and stewards of the mysteries of God." It goes on in verse 2 to say that we must be found faithful. God has trusted believers with information that is unknown to the rest of the world. In the last section, we discussed grace, which is one of the mysteries of which we are to be stewards. In this book, you have been learning about the mysteries of God's prosperity plan. This information is not currently known to those people who are operating in the worlds' plan; thus we must become good stewards of this information and use it properly. We are to put God's plan into action in our own lives, so that we can be examples of the prosperity that is available through Him. This will attract those who are operating in the world's system, as they will learn that God's plan has two benefits – both earthly and eternal prosperity. We are also to internalize God's plan and teach it to others – friends, family members, and particularly our children. God is unveiling many mysteries, which have been unknown to past generations. He expects us to be good stewards of this information.

God's Household

In the beginning, God created the earth and everything in it. He then gave dominion of it to mankind. We see this in Genesis 1:26, "Then God said, 'Let us make man in our image, in our likeness, and let them rule over the fish of the sea and the birds of the air, over the livestock, over all the earth and over all the creatures that move along the ground." God created paradise and put mankind in it to rule. In other words, He made us stewards of His household.

Jesus taught us to be good stewards of the Father's household in Luke 12:35-40, "Be dressed ready for service and keep your lamps burning, like men waiting for their master to return from a wedding banquet, so that when he comes and knocks they can immediately open the door for him. It will be good for those servants whose master finds them watching when he comes. I tell you the truth, he will dress himself to serve, will have them recline at the table and will come and wait on them. It will be good for those servants whose master finds them ready, even if he comes in the second or third watch of the night. But understand this: if the owner of the house had known what hour the thief was coming he would not have let his house be broken into. You also must be ready, because the Son of Man will come at an hour when you do not expect him."

Just like in this parable, we have been left as the stewards of God's household. One day, Jesus is going to return and wait upon those of us who are ready. So, we must be ready at all times. Strive to live a sinless life that is focused on the Lord, not the world. Operate daily in God's plan, not the world's plan. Be a good steward of the part of God's household that He has entrusted you with and He will reward you when He returns.

Areas of Stewardship

Although this book is focused on finances, God does give other resources of which He expects us to be good stewards; these include talents/gifts and time. In this section, you will learn how to be good stewards of all God-given resources.

Talents/Gifts

God has given every single person on earth talents and/or gifts. To some He has given great athletic abilities, which they are to use to glorify God. Kurt Warner, star quarterback for the St. Louis Rams is a great example of someone who has used his talent to glorify God. To others, God has given writing (C.S. Lewis) or speaking (Billy Graham) abilities, which they are to use to spread the good news of Jesus Christ as Savior. To others, God has given tremendous patience and the ability to work with children. If they are using their God-given gifts, they become teachers and daycare workers, where they can mold young lives for Christ. You have received talents; the only question is, do you know what they are? If so, are you using your talents to glorify God? Some day you will stand before God to give an account for how you used the talent He gave you. After the account, will He say, "Well done good and faithful servant?"

God also gives those who are already believers, spiritual gifts. These are outlined in Romans, 1st Corinthians, and Ephesians. Although there are many different gifts, they are all given by the same Spirit, according to 1st Corinthians 12:4. To determine your gifts, review 1st Corinthians 12:8-10, 1st Corinthians 12:28, Romans 12:6-8, and Ephesians 4:11. Here is a quick review of those verses. As you are reading them, determine which gifts God has given you.

1 Corinthians 12:8-10 tells us, "To one there is given through the Spirit the message of wisdom, to another the message of knowledge by means of the same Spirit, to another faith by the same Spirit, to another gifts of healing by that one Spirit, to another miraculous powers, to another prophecy, to another distinguishing between spirits (discernment), to another speaking in different tongues, and still another the interpretation of tongues." In these verses we see the following gifts: wisdom, knowledge, faith, healing, miracles, prophecy, discernment, tongues, and interpretation of tongues. Do any of these gifts jump out at you?

1 Corinthians 12:28 adds more spiritual gifts to our list. "And in the church, God has appointed first of all Apostles, second Prophets, third Teachers, then workers of miracles, also those having gifts of healing, those able to help others, those with gifts of administration, and those speaking in different kinds of tongues." Here you will find four new gifts – apostleship, teaching, helps, and administration.

Romans 12:6-8 shows us some additional gifts, "We have different gifts, according to the grace given us. If a man's gift is prophesying, let him use it in proportion to his faith. If it is serving, let him serve; if it is teaching, let him teach; if it is encouraging, let him encourage; if it is contributing to the needs of others, let him give generously; if it is leadership, let him govern diligently; if it is showing mercy, let him do it cheerfully." In these verses we see the following new gifts: service, teaching, encouragement (exhortation), contribution/giving, leadership, and mercy.

Ephesians 4:11 rounds out the spiritual gifts listed in the Bible, "It is he who gave some to be Apostles, some to be Prophets, some to be Evangelists, and some to be Pastors and Teachers." In this verse we find the final two gifts – evangelism and pasturing/ shepherding.

Have you received any of these gifts? If you are not sure, check with your Pastor to see if there is a spiritual gifts class or if they have a spiritual gifts test available. If not, check your local Christian bookstore for Your Spiritual Gifts by C. Peter Wagner. The book covers all the spiritual gifts and includes a good test.

One caution at this point: There are many churches and complete denominations that don't believe in the spiritual gifts or they believe that some of them have passed away. If you are part of a church like that, I challenge you to find anywhere in the Bible where it says that the spiritual gifts have passed away. It was the Apostle Paul who taught on the spiritual gifts and he was writing and speaking to the New Testament Church, of which all Christians are a part. If you have people telling you that speaking in tongues or healing or prophecy do not exist anymore, seek God's wisdom and not man's. God would not have allowed Paul to teach about the gifts and for them to have been included in the Bible, if they were not for us today.

Keys to Good Stewardship of Your Talents/Gifts

It is important to recognize the gifts that God has given you. It is even more important to learn how to be a good steward of those gifts. Here are the keys to good stewardship of your talents and gifts:

1. **When God gives spiritual gifts, it can cause problems with pride**. Some people begin thinking that they are better than others who do not have those gifts. Romans 12:3 says, "I say to every one of you: Do not think of yourself more highly than you ought, but rather think of yourself with sober judgment, in accordance with the measure of faith God has given you." God gives everyone gifts and He does not give them so that one person can be better than another. Instead, He gives gifts so that they can benefit the whole body of Christ. Examine your gifts, determine how they could be used to benefit others, and stay humble in the process.

2. **God intended all the gifts He gives to be used for the common good of all people**. 1 Corinthians 12:7 reads, "Now to each one the manifestation of the Spirit is given for the common good." God does not give us gifts that are to be used selfishly; rather they are to be used selflessly. We are all part of one body and just like your own body each part of you has a unique function. Eyes are to see. Feet are to be used to walk and dance. Hands are to be used to pick up things and clap. Just as each part of your body contributes to your ability to live life, each person in the church body has gifts that contribute to the good of the whole. Once you discover your gifts, you will be a greater contributor to the body of Christ.

3. **God gives us gifts in love and expects us to use them in love**. 1 Corinthians 13:1-3 says, "And now I will show you the most excellent way. If I speak in the tongues of men and of angels, but have not love, I am only a resounding gong or a clanging cymbal. If I have the gift of prophecy and can fathom all mysteries and all knowledge, and if I have a faith that can move mountains, but have not love, I

116

am nothing. If I give all I possess to the poor and surrender my body to the flames, but have not love I gain nothing." It is clear that love is the common denominator. The gifts are all different, but all should be administered with love.

4. **If we use our gifts properly, God will trust us with greater gifts.** We see this clearly in Matthew 13:12, "Whoever has will be given more and he will have abundance." God rewards good stewardship. As we identify and use our gifts properly, He will reward us with other gifts. These gifts when used properly will benefit all people and of course you will benefit as well. God expects that the gifts He gives us will enable us to live life abundantly.

Use Them or Lose Them

Gifts are like muscles, if you don't use them, they slowly diminish. However, just like working out in a gym will increase your muscle tone and size, using your spiritual gifts will increase them. So, it is important that we recognize our gifts and seek ways that we can use them regularly to benefit those around us.

If we do not use our gifts, a couple of things happen:

1. **We neglect God.** God gives us gifts for a purpose. When we don't use the gifts, we negate His purpose. Also, we must think about how it must grieve our heavenly Father, when we do not accept and use the gifts He gives us. How would it make you feel if you gave a gift to someone you love and they took the gift and threw it away right in front of you? Since we are made in God's image, it is likely that He has the same feelings when we throw away the incredible gifts He has given us.

2. **Quench the fire of the Holy Spirit.** God gives us gifts by the Holy Spirit. Along with each gift comes the power and authority to use that gift. The apostle Paul was trying to teach the Thessalonians this in 1 Thessalonians 5:19, "Do not put out the Spirit's fire; do not treat prophecies with contempt." Apparently the Thessalonians were negating the

gifts of the Spirit. This smothers the spiritual fire that is burning and stifles the work that God can do with each of us.

Time

The second area of stewardship is time. Although God gives us each different gifts, He gives us all exactly the same amount of time each day – 24 hours. What we do with that time shows our ability to be a good steward. How we use our time also shows our loyalty to either the world or to God.

How do you invest your time? How much of it is spent seeking God and His will for your life? How much of it is spent seeking what the world has to offer? Which do you think would be most beneficial? It's pretty obvious that the God of the universe would know more than we do about how we should invest the time He has given us. So, the key is to learn how to live in this busy world and yet seek God always. Here are some tips:

1. **Give your first fruits to God**. Just like you've already learned about tithing, God wants to be Lord over all parts of your life; this includes your time. So, each day tithe your time. In other words, give the first 10% of your day to God. When you wake up, instead of turning on the news, turn on some worship music and worship your creator. Invest time in the Bible every day, so that you can learn about God, His character, and His plan for you. While you are driving to work, leave the radio off and spend time in prayer; talking with God about the day. Find out what He wants you to do that day. Pray the prayer of Jabez each day, "Oh, that you would bless me and enlarge my territory! Let your hand be with me, and keep me from harm, so that I will be free from pain." (1 Chronicles 4:10) When Jabez prayed this prayer, the Bible says that God granted his request. When you invest the first hours of your day with God, He will grant your requests as well.

2. **Pray unceasingly**. Contrary to popular belief, you don't have to be in church on your hands and knees, with your

hands folded and eyes closed to pray. Prayer is nothing more than having a conversation with your best friend – Jesus or with your heavenly Father. If you have accepted Jesus, then you have the Holy Spirit living in you. Call on Him to help you pray, if you are not sure what to say. You can pray any time and anywhere. Pray in bed, the shower, your car, at the club, while mowing the lawn or doing laundry, at work, while fishing, and any other time you think about it, which should be often. Train yourself to pray throughout the day and you will draw close to God. This will enable you to hear Him better; enabling Him to share His prosperity plan for your life.

How we invest our time shows who or what is Lord of our life. If we invest more of our time with God, then we make Him Lord. On the other hand, if we spend more of our time in the world, dealing with worldly things, then we have made the world lord of our lives. Life never goes very well when the world is in control, because the world is temporarily controlled by Satan and is inherently evil. Oh, you will see people prosper in the world, but they never seem to be happy. Once they realize that money won't fill their emptiness, they often turn to alcohol and drugs to try to fill the void. We see their marriages and relationships fall apart. They are lonely, hopeless people who often take their own lives in desperation. Those who have made God the Lord of their lives have the joy of the Lord and they are content with their station in life, knowing that God is in control. So, who is Lord of your life? Which path you take will determine whether you are operating in the world's prosperity plan or God's. The choice is always yours!

Money/Finances

The third area of stewardship is money. A good portion of the Bible relates to money, finances, wealth, or riches. Jesus had many teachings about money. We are going to look at two of these in this section. The first is the Parable of the Talents, which you will find in Matthew 25, verses 14-

30. "Again, it will be like a man going on a journey, who called his servants and entrusted his property to them. To one he gave five talents of money, to another two talents, and to another one talent, each according to his ability. Then he went on his journey. The man who had received the five talents went at once and put his money to work and gained five more. So also, the one with the two talents gained two more. But the man who had received the one talent went off, dug a hole in the ground and hid his master's money."

"After a long time the master of those servants returned and settled the accounts with them. The man who had received the five talents brought the other five. 'Master,' he said, 'you entrusted me with five talents. See, I have gained five more.' His master replied, 'Well done, good and faithful servant! You have been faithful with a few things; I will put you in charge of many things. Come and share your master's happiness!' The man with two talents also came. 'Master,' he said, 'you entrusted me with two talents; see, I have gained two more.' His master replied, 'Well done, good and faithful servant! You have been faithful with a few things; I will put in charge of many things. Come and share your master's happiness!' Then the man who had received the one talent came. 'Master,' he said, 'I knew that you are a hard man, harvesting where you have not sown and gathering where you have not scattered seed. So I was afraid and went out and hid your talent in the ground. See, here is what belongs to you.' His master replied, 'You wicked, lazy servant! So you knew that I harvest where I have not sown and gather where I have not scattered seed? Well then, you should have put my money on deposit with the bankers, so that when I returned I would have received it back with interest. Take the talent from him and give it to the one who has the ten talents. For everyone who has will be given more and he will have an abundance. Whoever does not have, even what he has will be taken from him. And throw that worthless servant outside, into the darkness, where there will be weeping and gnashing of teeth.'"

There are many things we can learn from this parable. First, in the parable, God is the master and we are the servants. According to verse 15, God has given us some of his money. When He returns (when Jesus returns to claim the earth), He expects us to have been good stewards of His money. We do not know when He will return, so it's important that we stay focused on being good stewards. We also see in verse 15 that we are each given an amount according to our ability. Those who have shown that they can handle small amounts that God has given them are then entrusted with greater amounts.

In verses 16-17 we learn that God expects us to put His money to work for increase. As was discussed earlier, part of the money He gives us is meant to be planted into good ministry works. We must tithe and give, so that God can provide a harvest. The rest of the money is ours to use as we choose. However, since it's all God's money, He does expect us to use our part wisely; creating increase.

In verse 18 we see that there will be some people who are entrusted with God's money, who operate in fear, instead of faith. They do nothing with the money and so God does not have an opportunity to create an increase.

In verses 19-23, we see the reward that is in store for those of us who are good stewards of God's money. First, we receive benefit here on earth, in that we get to keep the increase. Plus, as we show that we are good stewards of a little, God will give us more. These verses have double meaning as well. We will not only be put in charge of more while here on earth, but once the new heaven is established here on earth (see Revelation 21) we will be given greater responsibilities and will revel in God's joy.

Verse 26 shows us that God will punish lazy stewards. Those people who are not good stewards will have the money they have been given taken away. Self-centered people will be judged, as their hearts were not given to the Lord. They were focused on themselves, which means they will be cast away from God into the darkness, where there is great pain and agony. Keep in mind that God does everything possible and gives each person every possible chance to show that God is truly Lord of his or her life. He is not a punishing God. He is a loving God and wants all of His children to reside in the new heaven for the rest of eternity, enjoying His abundance and joy. It is each persons choice as to whether they are good stewards of their talents, time, and money by making God Lord of their lives or if they choose to be selfish and focus on their own needs, thus ignoring God and making the world (and the devil) Lord of their lives.

Verses 28 and 29 show us that the wealth of the wicked and lazy will be transferred to the wise and the righteous and that we will all enjoy God's abundance (both here on earth and later in heaven). Verse 29 shows us that if we are faithful with the little that God gives us, He will trust us with more. God really wants to pour abundant prosperity out into the lives of His children; however, he doesn't want to ruin lives by pouring it out when people are not prepared. Have you been faithful with the little that God has given you or have you gotten caught in the traps of the world and are in debt? If you are caught in the world's snare, it's not too late; there is still time before the master returns. Use this book to get yourself out of debt and become a good steward of the money that God entrusts you with. Then some day you will stand in front of God and He will say, "Well done, good and faithful servant! You have been faithful with a few things; I will put you in charge of many things. Come and share your master's happiness!" That will be a glorious day.

Jesus teaches us about the other side of stewardship – greed, in the Parable of the Rich Fool (Luke 12:15-21). This is why God is very careful not to pour out massive prosperity on people until they are ready. Here is the parable: "'Watch out! Be on your guard against all kinds of greed; a man's life does not consist in the abundance of his possessions.' And he told them this parable: The ground of a certain rich man produced a good crop. He thought to himself, 'What shall I do? I have no place to store my crops.' Then he said, 'This is what I'll do. I will tear down my barns and build bigger ones, and there I will store all my grain and my goods. And I'll say to myself, you have plenty of good things laid up for many years. Take life easy; eat, drink and be merry.' But God said to him, 'You fool! This very night your life will be demanded from you. Then who will get what you have prepared for yourself?' This is how it will be with anyone who stores up things for himself, but is not rich toward God."

This story teaches us two lessons. First, we must be on constant guard against greed. It can strike at any time; even when you only have a little. If your focus is on the money and getting more; and you are not giving to God, then you are operating in a spirit of greed. Second, our focus should always be on what we can do for God with the money He has given us. If our focus is continually on God's work and we are using the money He has given us to further the Kingdom, then He will reward us with more and we will enjoy abundance here on earth, as well as in the eternal life after death.

Focus on God, Not Money

Money itself is not inherently good or bad; it is just a thing that we give value to here on earth. Yes, it is very necessary in our lives and God recognizes this. However, it should not be our focus. Satan wants you to be focused on money and the world's system for getting more of it, so you can have status in the world. God wants you to focus on Him and His work and when you do, He will provide prosperity as you are ready.

For many years, the church and religious people have been operating in error about money. They have been saying, "Money is the root of all evil." Many people believe that the Bible actually says this, when it doesn't! In his first letter to Timothy (1 Timothy 6:10) the apostle Paul writes, "For the <u>love of money</u> is the root of all kinds of evil. Some people, eager for money, have wandered from the faith and pierced themselves with many griefs." Clearly the concern here is not money, but focus. People who are focused on money wander away from their faith in God, thus making the world (and Satan) lord of their lives.

A recent graduate of the God's Prosperity Plan course is an attorney who for many years was focused on money. He had grown up in a poor family and was determined to never be poor again. Even after he had secured his financial life, he would have nightmares about not having enough money, so he would strive even harder to bring in more money. However, the more he focused on money, the emptier he got, until the day the Spirit of God called him and he answered by giving his heart to the Lord. A few months later he attended the G.P.P. class and struggled with the teaching. It was hard for him to commit to the tithe and giving on top, but as the Lord softened his heart, he committed to God's plan. This opened his heart to the Lord's instruction. God told him to sell his house and payoff all his debt so he could faithfully tithe and give at least 10% above the tithe. When he told friends about God's plan, they thought he was crazy. However God showed Himself mighty as the plan unfolded. The house was listed on a Friday and on Monday he had a full price offer. The house closed less than thirty days later. He is now debt free and fulfilling his part of the deal by tithing and giving 10% and God continues to bless him abundantly in all parts of his life.

If your focus is on money, you will never have enough to make you happy. Ecclesiastes 5:10 says, "Whoever loves money never has money enough; whoever loves wealth is never satisfied with his income." We've all encountered people who have more money than they could spend in their lifetime and yet they are still working to make more. No matter how much money they seem to have, they are never truly happy. This is because money and material things can only result in temporary happiness, not the true joy that we are all seeking. Only turning your life completely over to Jesus will result in true joy.

The problem is that money is a master and as Jesus said in Luke 16:13, "No servant can serve two masters. Either he will hate the one and love the other, or he will be devoted to the one and despise the other. You cannot serve both God and Money." We put so much value on money, because it is a major focal point of the world's system. However, as we continue on to the last part of verse 15, Jesus said, "What is highly valued among men is detestable in God's sight." Money means nothing to God. He wants us to be focused on Him, not on money.

Jesus made it very simple in Matthew 6:33 when he said, "But seek first his kingdom and his righteousness, and all these things will be given to you as well." The things Jesus was referring to were food, drink, clothes, and a place to live. If we seek God first and keep our eyes on Him, He will provide all that we need. In fact, according to 2 Chronicles 26:5, if we seek God we will prosper and if we meditate on His Word day and night, we will be successful and prosperous.

Give Back to God

God loved us so much that He gave us His only Son, that if we believe in Him, we are saved from the punishment that is due us, because of our sin. Also, He has blessed us with talents, gifts, time, and money. Shouldn't we be giving back to God? In regards to our money, we are to tithe (first 10% of our income and increase). This shows that God is Lord of our finances and is an act of obedience that God will bless. As we learned earlier in this book, if we tithe we receive a blessing and God protects the other 90% from the devourer (Malachi 3:10-12). If we don't tithe, we are robbing God and are under a curse (Malachi 3:8-9). Set aside the first

10% of your income and any increase and take it into the storehouse (your church) each week.

You are probably wondering why we keep covering the tithe and repeating the same scriptures? It is because the tithe is such a critical part of God's prosperity plan. Think of the tithe as the key that starts God's prosperity machine. If you don't have a key, then you can't participate in the plan and miss out on the blessings. So, since we believe that repetition will help you to remember the important things, we will continue to hammer home the issue of the tithe.

The tithe is only the beginning. It is just giving God back what is already His. If we go beyond the tithe and give Him gifts, we show our love for Him. As you learned earlier in 2nd Corinthians 9:7, God loves a cheerful giver. Do you give cheerfully to God? God also loves to bless generous givers. Proverbs 11:25 reads, "A generous man will prosper . . ." Proverbs 22:11 says, "A generous man will himself be blessed . . ." God blesses generous givers using His own measure, according to Luke 6:38. Are you giving a little and expecting a lot back? He gave up His only Son for us. How much that must have hurt! Are you giving back to Him until it hurts or are you giving what you have left over?

We witnessed a great example of this at a men's conference a few years ago. A young man, I (Rod) had been discipling, drove from his home in Canada to Tacoma, WA for the conference. His income was very limited, so we paid his conference fees, provided him with a place to stay and meals. The Holy Spirit was very strong at the conference and at one point the young man felt the Lord telling him to give all the money he had in an offering. He argued with God over night, as by doing so, he would not have enough money to get home. After a sleepless night, he arrived at the conference and gave all that he had (around $20). During the next two hours, three men came up to the young man and handed him wads of cash, saying that God had told them to give the money to him. He ended up with about triple what he had given. He gave until it hurt (all he had) and then trusted God to take care of his needs. God was and always is faithful!

Now is the time to make changes and start making God Lord of your finances. How you spend your money shows God how much you love and are devoted to Him. Are you giving until it hurts and then trusting God to take care of your needs or do you still trust in the world's system?

Your Stewardship Plan

In this chapter, you have learned a lot about stewardship. Now it's time to create your own stewardship plan:

1. **Repent of any sin in your life**. God cannot bless you with un-confessed sin. (Proverbs 28:13).

2. **Get your eyes on Jesus**. God cannot bless you if you are focused on the financial storms around you. (Matthew 6:33 and 14:28-30)

3. **Free yourself of scarcity mentality**. Remember the steward who buried the talent out of fear. God wants you to have abundance. Read and speak God's prosperity promises into your life every day. Jesus came to give us abundant life (John 10:10).

4. **Become a person who consistently tithes**. Get excited about writing the first check (10%) to God. You will be amazed at how much farther the other 90% goes each month. (Malachi 3:8-12)

5. **Become a generous and cheerful giver**. Put yourself on a monthly giving program. For example, you might tithe the first 10% and give another 10%, then increase it 1% each month. By doing this, you will be exercising and building up your faith muscle. (Proverbs 11:25, 2 Corinthians 9:7)

6. **Eliminate debt**. Debt is a tool of the enemy that he has used to bind us for years. It keeps people bound and unable to tithe and give. Develop a budget so that you can live on 70% of your income or less. Begin paying off debt. God

wants you to be debt-free. By reducing your debt and keeping your living expenses the same, you will then have more money available to give, which means God will be able to bless you even more! (Proverbs 22:7)

7. **Reduce your living expenses**. Where you spend your money shows your loyalty. Do you spend more money in the world or do you give more to God? Who is truly Lord of your life? If it's not God right now, then ask for His forgiveness and divine wisdom to get yourself to a point where you are giving God more than you spend in the world.

8. **Invest to create an increase**. If you are planting the seed God has given you into good ministry ground, then it will create an abundant harvest in the spiritual realm. God will also cause increase in the physical realm to benefit your life. Plus, God expects us to use the other 90% to create increase. Ask God to lead you to good investments where the wealth of the wicked can begin to flow over to you. Then tithe and give off the increase that God creates. God wants all of us to begin working on a plan that maintains our standard of living, but constantly increases our income, so that at some point in the near future, we will be able to live (very nicely) off the 10% and give away the other 90% to further God's Kingdom.

9. **Find ways to increase your earning potential**. God is unlimited, but sometimes we limit Him with our limited income jobs. Look for ways you can improve your skills and knowledge, so that you can qualify for a promotion or better paying job. Start a side business to create another stream of income. However, always keep in mind that God is your source, not the job, business, or investments. Don't get so focused on the money that you forget God.

10. **As God blesses you, remember to give Him the credit and thank Him**. Nothing good can come from us, unless God is there. Thank Him daily for your blessings. Give credit where it is due and you will glorify the One who has blessed you.

God gives us each talents, gifts, time, and money. He expects us to be good stewards of those resources, until He returns. We don't know when that will be, so we need to utilize our talents, gifts, time and money to advance the Kingdom every single day. Some day you will stand before your Creator and give an account for how you used the resources He gave you. This we know for sure. The only question is what will be His response to your account. Will it be "You wicked, lazy servant" or "Well done my good and faithful servant." The choice is yours!

Chapter Six Discussion Questions

1. What is a steward? Discuss examples.

2. What are the overall areas of stewardship? Discuss each.

3. What is the "manifold grace of God?"

4. What are the "mysteries of God?"

5. What is included in "God's household?"

6. What three things does God expect you to be a steward over? How are you doing?

7. What talents has God given you and how are you using them to glorify God?

8. What spiritual gifts has God given you and how are you using them to glorify God?

9. What are the four keys to good stewardship of your talents and gifts?

10. How are you using your time? Is it glorifying to God?

11. How are you handling the money God gives you? Is it glorifying Him?

12. Are you focused on money or God? Discuss the differences.

Seven

Seek Wisdom and
Wealth Will Follow

Chapter 7

Seek Wisdom and Wealth Will Follow

The world's prosperity plan will tell you to seek wealth. Go down to your local book store and look at the number of books on wealth. They are all saying the same thing: focus your mind on an amount of money you want to attain, set goals, and move into action. Those are all good things except that they forgot the most important point – seek God's will; the One who is all knowing and all powerful. God knows whether you are ready for wealth and if so, exactly what you need to do to attract it. Focus your eyes on God, seek His wisdom, and wealth will chase you down. If you chase after wealth, it will flee from you.

The person who understood this best was Solomon. As you learned earlier, he had the unique opportunity to receive from God anything he wanted (1 Kings 3:5). Solomon could have told God that he wanted great wealth, but instead he asked for wisdom. This pleased God and He not only gave Solomon extreme wisdom, but also riches, honor, and long life. Solomon became incredibly wealthy. So great was the wealth in his kingdom that silver was no more valuable than the pebbles in the street (1 Chronicles 1:15). He understood that if you go to God for wisdom, wealth will follow.

So, what is wisdom and how do we get it? In order to gain a better understanding, let's examine a couple of definitions for wisdom:

1. **Reader's Digest Encyclopedia Dictionary** – "The power of true and right discernment; also conformity to the course of action dictated by such discernment." In this definition, we see two key concepts. The first is discernment and the second is a course of action. Discernment is defined

as the act or process of exhibiting keen insight and good judgment. So, the keys here are to have the ability to have insight into a situation and then develop the appropriate course of action.

2. **Layman's Bible Encyclopedia** – "Skill in making application of thoughts to actions; a gift from God stemming from right relationship with Him." In this definition there are three keys. The first is making application of thoughts, which would equate to discernment. The second is action, so wisdom is not just thought, but rather thoughts put into action. Third, wisdom is a gift from God that results from having an intimate relationship with Him. Solomon was mentioned earlier in this chapter. The Bible indicates that he was the wisest man on earth and might possibly have been the wisest man in history. His wisdom was a result of his relationship with God. 1 Kings 3:3 says, "And Solomon loved the Lord. . ."

How is your relationship with God? Are you like Solomon and love the Lord or is God a stranger to you? Many people spend years in church learning about God, but never really know Him. If you don't know your heavenly Father, invest time every day reading His Holy Word – the Bible. Ask God to show Himself through His Word. Tell the Lord that you would like to develop a close relationship with Him; that you seek His wisdom for your life. He will answer. Deuteronomy 4:29 says, "But if from there you seek the Lord your God, you will find him if you look for him with all your heart and with all your soul." Proverbs 8:17 reads, "I love those who love me, and those who seek me find me." Jeremiah 29:13 says, "You will seek me and find me when you seek me with all your heart." God is waiting to have a relationship with you and to give you His wisdom.

Many people think that wisdom is following the laws of God, also known as the Ten Commandments. Although these are very important rules to follow, in themselves they are not wisdom. No set of rules can cover all situations, so

God has given us the ability to make choices in every situation. For best results, seek God ahead of time before making those choices and he will give you His wisdom for that situation. James 1:5 says, "If any of you lacks wisdom, he should ask God, who gives generously without finding fault, and it will be given to him." As you encounter life's challenges and seek God's wisdom, you will learn. When you don't seek God's wisdom and go on your own, you will also learn valuable (and sometimes painful) lessons. These experiences also contribute to your wisdom.

Some people think that wisdom is knowledge, but we've all encountered incredibly intelligent people who make stupid decisions that dramatically affect their lives. Knowledge in itself is not wisdom, however it is a contributor. This is another reason to invest time reading the Bible every day and seeking God's wisdom through meditation on the Word and in prayer. The more knowledge you gain about God, His character, and His ways, the greater the chance you will react properly when the storms of life blow your way. Jesus teaches this in Matthew 7:24-27, "Therefore everyone who hears these words of mine and puts them into practice is like a wise man who built his house on the rock. The rain came down, the streams rose, and the winds blew and beat against that house; yet it did not fall, because it had its foundation on the rock. But everyone who hears these words of mine and does not put them into practice is like a foolish man who built his house on sand. The rain came down, the streams rose, and the winds blew and beat against that house, and it fell with a great crash." When you read God's Word and plant it into your heart, you build your house on the rock. When you go through life without God, you build your house on the sand. Start today, building your house on the solid rock of Jesus Christ!

OK, now that you know about wisdom and why you should have it, you are probably wondering how to gain more of it. There are three means to gain wisdom:

1. **Fear God** – Proverbs 9:10 reads, "The fear of the Lord is the beginning of wisdom . . ." What does it mean to fear the Lord? Are we supposed to be afraid that He will get us? Many people have this view of God; that He has a big club and is ready to bonk them on the head every time they do something wrong. First, this is not true. Our God is a loving God, who sent His Son, Jesus, to die for us, so that He could once again enjoy an intimate relationship with us. He is a loving Father reaching toward us with open arms, who seeks relationship with each of us. Second, we are not talking about the type of fear where you are afraid of something or someone. The Hebrew word, which translates as fear in our English Bible, is Yirah (yir-aw'), which means respect, awe, or reverence. We are to be in awe of God and revere Him. After all, He is all knowing and all-powerful. He is the creator of the universe and all of us. Shouldn't we be in awe of that and approach Him with reverence? In our day-to-day lives we show God respect by seeking Him first in all aspects of our lives. As we read earlier, Matthew 6:33 says, "But seek first his kingdom . . ." Those who fear God, seek Him first for His will and His plan; then are willing to obey. Many people say they fear God, but they go on with their own plans, never seeking God's perfect will for their life. It comes down to a heart issue, not a knowledge issue. You can't even begin the path to gaining wisdom without reverence for God.

2. **Seek God and Ask** – Luke 11:9 reads, "So I say to you: Ask and it will be given to you; seek and you will find; knock and the door will be opened to you." Seek God with your whole heart and ask Him for wisdom. Most people are either too afraid to ask God or don't think that He hears their requests. God is like a good Father, He hears every request from His children. The key is that God is a gentleman. He does not force things upon His kids; rather, He waits until we ask. So, if we want our lives to go well, particularly our financial lives, we need to be seeking God and asking Him for His wisdom in every situation. It's important that when

you ask for God's wisdom and He gives it, that you don't doubt. James 1:5-8 reads, "If any of you lacks wisdom, he should ask God, who gives generously to all without finding fault, and it will be given to him. But when he asks, he must believe and not doubt, because he who doubts is like a wave of the sea, blown and tossed by the wind. That man should not think he will receive anything from the Lord; he is a double-minded man, unstable in all he does." When God gives you His wisdom, believe and obey; you will be blessed.

3. **Meditate on the Word** – We have discussed the importance of this several times throughout this book. God wrote the Bible through various writers. Hebrews 4:12 says, "For the Word of God is living and active." Although the Bible was written thousands of years ago, it is still the living Word of God and useful instruction for your life. God is looking for people who know Him in their heart. 2 Chronicles 16:9 reads, "For the eyes of the Lord run to and fro throughout the whole earth, to show Himself strong on behalf of those whose heart is loyal to Him." God is looking for people who want His wisdom and are reading and meditating on His Word, because He knows that without reading His instruction manual (**B**asic **I**nstructions **B**efore **L**eaving **E**arth), we cannot possibly know His way or will for our life. If we do not read and meditate on the Word, we are forced to follow the world's way, which will eventually lead us to destruction. Psalm 1:1-6 confirms the answer, "Blessed is the man who does not walk in the counsel of the wicked or stand in the way of sinners or sit in the seat of mockers. But his delight is in the law of the Lord (Bible), and on his law he meditates day and night. He is like a tree planted by streams of water, which yields its fruit in season and whose leaf does not whither. <u>Whatever he does prospers</u>." Wouldn't you like to have everything in your life prosper? If so, then do what it says - read and meditate on the Bible every day.

Now you know what wisdom is and how to gain it, you may still be wondering why you would want wisdom. Here are some of the benefits of wisdom:

1. **Accurate Judgment** - In 1st Kings, chapter 3, we see God coming to Solomon and telling him he can have anything he wants. This is kind of like the old genie-in-a-bottle story, where the guy gets 3 wishes, except that Solomon only got one. He had to choose right. Fortunately, Solomon had grown up with the Word planted firmly in his heart and he had wisdom. The result was accurate judgment – he asked God for more wisdom. God gave him wisdom and included a few bonuses - wealth, health, and long life. The obvious thing for Solomon to ask for was wealth, but he had insight beyond the obvious. By gaining God's wisdom, you too will have insight beyond the obvious. You will make better relationship, business, and financial decisions, because God will let you see what others can't.

2. **Success In Everything You Do** – Because Solomon asked for wisdom, God gave him greater wisdom than any man who has ever lived on the earth. This wisdom led to tremendous success in all parts of his life. He brought peace to Israel; was known as the wisest man of his times; and had the greatest wealth of anyone on earth. Most importantly, he had a right relationship with God. He experienced success in all areas of his life. Instead of focusing on money and material things, as the world does, ask God for wisdom. His wisdom will result in wealth beyond your wildest dreams. Not only will you enjoy wealth, but God promises success in everything you do – business, relationships, finances, and so on. People will look upon your life and see an example of God's favor and blessing. Seek wisdom and success will chase you down.

3. **Honor from God and Man** – In 1st Kings 10 we see that wisdom resulted in God honoring Solomon. God blessed every aspect of Solomon's life. Because Solomon operated in the favor of God, he was also honored by man. The

Queen of Sheba had heard about Solomon's wisdom and wealth, so she came to see for herself. She honored Solomon by bringing incredible gifts – 120 talents (4-1/2 tons) of gold, large quantities of spices, and precious stones. 1 Kings 10: 24-25 says, "The whole world sought audience with Solomon to hear the wisdom God had put in his heart. Year after year, everyone who came brought a gift - articles of silver and gold, robes, weapons and spices, and horses and mules." Clearly, Solomon was honored by both God and man. Solomon was no better, in God's eyes than you are. When you ask for God's wisdom and are obedient, you too will be favored by both God and man; everything you do will succeed.

4. **Wealth and Riches** – 1 Kings 10:23 reads, "King Solomon was greater in riches and wisdom than all the other kings of the earth." He had fourteen hundred chariots, which would be like having fourteen hundred cars in today's world. He also had twelve thousand horses. Gold was so common in his Kingdom, that there was no need to use silver, so they just threw it out in the streets like stones. Wealth was the result of the wisdom Solomon received from God. We need to stop seeking wealth in the world and start seeking wisdom from God. Wealth follows wisdom.

5. **Knowledge Beyond Your Years** – By seeking God's wisdom through His Word (Bible), we gain knowledge beyond that of the average man or woman. Psalm 119:97-100 reads, "Oh, how I love your law! I meditate on it all day long. Your commands make me wiser than my enemies for they are ever with me. I have more insight than all my teachers, for I meditate on your statutes. I have more understanding than the elders for I obey your precepts." God is all-knowing, so as we tap into His knowledge base, by meditating on the Word, we gain knowledge that takes us way beyond our years. This knowledge will enable you to create wealth and also to avoid sin and destructive living. You always have a choice – you can learn things through the school of hard knocks, which of course will be painful and

will take a great deal of time to gain knowledge or you can seek the wisdom of God and quickly gain tremendous knowledge without the pain. Which way will you choose?

6. **Enjoyment in Life and Healthy Relationships** – As we have all encountered, there are very few people who are truly enjoying life and have healthy relationships. Ecclesiastes 2:24-26 says, "A man can do nothing better than to eat and drink and find satisfaction in his work. This too, I see, is from the hand of God, for without him, who can eat or find enjoyment? To the man who pleases him, God gives wisdom, knowledge and happiness, but to the sinner he gives the task of gathering and storing up wealth to hand it over to the one who pleases God." God's wisdom enables us to avoid many of the troubles in the world and to truly find enjoyment of life. God's wisdom enables us to better understand people and their needs, which allows us to serve them better, resulting in healthy relationships.

7. **Balance in Life** – One of the most difficult tasks we have in life is balance. Each of us has been given 24 hours a day. The world is constantly tugging at us and trying to use up our time. God's wisdom enables us to better understand the priorities in life, which allows us to use our time more efficiently. The Bible says that there is a time for everything (Ecclesiastes 3:1-13). The key is to seek God for His timing, not to struggle through life using our own limited wisdom.

As you have likely surmised, wisdom can dramatically change every aspect of your life. Seek God's wisdom by meditating over His Word every day; by investing time with Him in prayer; by attending Spirit-filled church services and classes; and by fellowshipping with other Spirit-filled Christians. Don't be like the people of the world who are trying to do things with their own wisdom, but rather be like Jesus and seek God's wisdom regarding everything you do, every day and wealth will flow into your life so abundantly, that you will not have enough room for all of it and maybe for the first time in your life, you will truly enjoy your life; not because of the wealth, but because of the loving relationship you have with your Creator and heavenly Father.

Chapter Seven Discussion Questions

1. What is wisdom? Discuss the differences between wisdom from God and the world.

2. What are the three means for gaining wisdom? Discuss each.

3. What are the benefits of wisdom? Discuss each.

4. Why is accurate judgment important in this crazy world?

5. One of the benefits of wisdom is success – what does that look like in your life?

6. Discuss what it would mean in your life to be honored by God and man.

7. If God heaped riches on you, as He did with Solomon, what would be the impact?

8. How would wise knowledge be beneficial to you?

9. How might God's wisdom help you in your relationships?

10. What would have to happen in order for you to feel in complete balance?

11. What is your plan for gaining more wisdom from this point on?

Eight

Surviving Until Prosperity Arrives

Chapter 8

Surviving Until Prosperity Arrives

In the first seven chapters of this book, you have learned everything you need to know in order to enjoy the benefits of God's prosperity plan. You learned about His divine plan and the qualifications for tapping into the plan. You also learned how to develop a prosperity mindset and the powerful principles of sowing and reaping. Then you learned that partnering with God comes with privileges and how to become a good steward of what God has given and will give you. In the chapter you just completed, you learned to seek wisdom and wealth would follow.

If you have read all the chapters to this point and have put all the principles into operation in your life, then you are fully operating in God's plan. Unlike the world's plan that promises immediate results, but can't deliver, God's plan may take time. Remember that we are operating in His time frame, not ours. So, in the balance of this chapter, you will learn what to do while you are waiting for prosperity to arrive.

All of the keys can be found in Exodus 14:13, "And Moses said to the people, 'Do not be afraid. Stand still, and see the salvation of the Lord, which He will accomplish for you today." The context of this scripture was that the Israelites were backed up to the Red Sea with the Egyptian army bearing down on them. Sometimes in life it seems that your back is against the wall and the troubles of the world are bearing down on you. Let's study this scripture and see what we can learn.

The first part of the scripture reads, "And Moses said to the people, 'Don't be afraid.'" So, our first key, while we are waiting for prosperity to arrive, is to not be afraid.

Key #1: Don't Be Afraid

It is during this time of waiting that the deceiver will come against you. He will use friends, family members, partners, and co-workers to do his work. They will tell you that life will never be any different and that you will always live paycheck-to-paycheck. They'll tell you that you're too old or too young or that you don't have enough education to be prosperous. They'll try to steal your dreams, so beware of the dream stealers. Oh, they think they mean well, but are motivated by evil forces and this advice will be harmful to your life. Ephesians 6:12 says, "For our struggle is not against flesh and blood, but against the rulers, against the authorities, against the powers of this dark world and against spiritual forces of evil in the heavenly realms." Don't get upset with the people in your life that come against you, but rather do battle with the evil forces that are motivating them. Continuing on in Ephesians 6, you will learn about the armor of God and how to do battle in the spiritual realm. The real key here is not to allow fear to come in and cause you to go your own way and out of God's will.

There are different types of fear and in this case, we are not talking about the type of fear that you might experience if you were in the woods and a bear attacked you. Rather this is the fear of the unknown. Since you are waiting for an invisible God to deliver something you have never experienced (extreme prosperity), fear and doubt may try to creep into your mind. Best selling author, Denis Waitley has a great way of looking at this type of fear:

F = False

E = Expectations

A = Appearing

R = Real

The type of fear you may experience at this stage of the plan will appear as false expectations appearing real. Have you ever thought through a future situation so thoroughly that your stomach was in knots, you were perspiring, and your heart was racing, even though the expectations were not real? Fear creates pictures in your mind, which then results in emotions, which often turns into actions. This means that you are acting on something that isn't real. Many people miss out on God's prosperity because they begin doubting and start to take control of the situation again. This always leads to disaster and a blockage of God's flow of prosperity.

The interesting thing is that fear and excitement create the same bodily reactions – a pit in your stomach, sweaty palms, and a racing heart. So, you can interpret your situation and how you are feeling as either fear or excitement. Let's examine whether we should be fearful or excited while waiting for prosperity to arrive. Ask yourself this question: *Has God promised you prosperity, if you tap into His prosperity plan and give Him control?* If you have done all the things He has been telling you to do, in order to enter into His plan, then the answer is a resounding YES! If this is true, then you should be incredibly excited, because God must always fulfill His promises and you are going to experience prosperity.

Here are a few tips for avoiding fear, doubt, and even panic during this waiting period:

1. **Know the prosperity promises of God**. We have given you a number of them in this book. Read them over and over, until they are internalized. That way, when the devil comes against you with his lies; you can shut him up by speaking the truth of the Word of God.

2. **Know that God is always bigger than your circumstances**. Your debt load may seem like a mountain and the bill collectors are calling daily, but God is still bigger. God works through your faith. If you don't believe, He is unable to work in your life. Keep your eyes focused on Him and He will deliver you from the storm. Remember in Matthew 14 when Peter saw Jesus walking on the water. He called out to Jesus, "Lord, if it's you, tell me to come to

you on the water." Jesus told him to "Come" and Peter began doing something that seemed impossible; he began walking on the water toward Jesus. As long as Peter kept his eyes on Jesus, he defied the natural laws. When Peter took his eyes off Jesus and began looking at the storm and the waves, he began to sink. It's the same for you when the storms are raging all around you and things look bleak, keep your eyes on Jesus and He will supernaturally defy your circumstances.

3. **Know that it's God's timing, not yours**. God is all knowing and we are not, so it's actually better that He's the one dictating the timing or we would mess it up every time. We have many, many stories of students who were in dire financial need and God provided exactly what they needed in the 11th hour. When you are operating in God's plan, He will take care of all your needs, as He is preparing to move your financial prosperity from the spiritual realm to the physical realm. It is so important for you to be patient and let God do His work. Your job is to wait and trust in God. Have confidence that He will provide prosperity into your life in His timing, which is the right time.

4. **If there isn't enough money to take care of your needs, seek God for wisdom**. Invest some time in prayer and meditation. Ask God why there isn't enough money. Perhaps you will need to eliminate some expenses or He will reveal a way to earn some additional money. Just recently Karen and I (Rod) were concerned about the upcoming cost of Christmas. We had started a savings account in January and had the money saved, but an unexpected tax bill emptied that account and we were left with very little for Christmas. We are never very lavish with presents, but with five children and three grandchildren, a little for each really adds up. As I was praying one morning, the Lord told me to sell some things I didn't need. I looked around my office and realized I had a couple old computers, a disk drive, and a printer. I quickly listed those on e-bay and within seven days had generated exactly the amount that we needed for

Christmas. The interesting thing is that I had tried to sell some of those items a year earlier and no one even bid on them. This time, they sold for more than I expected. The key was God's timing. He knows all and no matter what your circumstance, He will provide you with the solution that is within His will.

5. **Be content with what God has given you**. The world we live in is so materially focused. God didn't promise you a mansion and Mercedes, but He did promise to take care of all your needs. This doesn't mean that God won't give you a mansion and a Mercedes, but that's His choice, not ours. Focus on Him and then be patient. There are two Greek words that translate into the English word patience. The first is "hupomone" (hoop-om-on-ay') which means quality of endurance under trials and free from discouragement. The second Greek word is "makrothumia" (mak-orth-oo-mee'-ah) which means endurance and steadfastness. God wants us to have both types of patience, as we wait on the prosperity that He has promised. Talk about patience, I (Tim) had waited forty years for a wife. Many times I had lamented to God about not having a wife and He told me to be patient. In His timing, God brought a wonderful woman into my life and I was prepared to ask for her hand in marriage. The only problem was that I had recently jumped into full-time ministry and so my income was somewhat sporadic and I didn't have enough to pay for the engagement ring. During my prayer time, God assured me that He would provide the money. I ordered the ring through a relative who is a jewelry broker and she was just waiting for the payment. The day I had scheduled was now just a few days away and still no money. I was continuing to pray and God was continuing to assure me. The day before the payment was due a gentleman I had recently met and ministered to, walked into the office and handed me an envelope. He told me that God had told him to give this to me for an impending financial need. I thanked him and after he left, opened the envelope and inside was a check for exactly what I needed for the ring. Praise

the Lord! When we are in God's will and remain patient, He will always provide.

6. **God may be testing your patience**. God never tempts us, but He does test us at times to see if we are ready for prosperity. As we said earlier in the book, God doesn't want to destroy His kid's lives with prosperity, so He won't provide it until we are ready. 2 Corinthians 6:6 says, "We have proved ourselves by our purity, our understanding, our patience, our kindness, our sincere love, and the power of the Holy Spirit." Prove to God that you have the patience necessary and prosperity will arrive into your life.

7. **Persevere through the trials**. Jesus said that there would be tribulation in life. He also said that the thief comes to steal, kill and destroy. The devil has an evil plan for your life and he will put you through many trials. James 1:2-4 says, "Consider it pure joy, my brother, whenever you face trials of many kinds, because you know that the testing of your faith develops perseverance. Perseverance must finish its work so that you may be mature and complete, not lacking anything." God uses the trials to build us up, so that we are ready for the responsibilities of prosperity. When faced with a trial, get excited, God is at work in you.

Ok, let's go back to Exodus 14:13 for the second key: "Stand still." The Hebrew word that translates into stand is "yatsab" which means to present or station oneself.

Key #2: Stand

While God is at work bringing prosperity into your life, present or station yourself to do anything He asks. Here are a few things we know we should be doing while we are standing:

1. **No complaining**. Philippians 2:14 says, "In everything you do, stay away from complaining . . ." After God delivered them from slavery the Israelites complained about their hardships out in the desert and it took them 40 years to make an 11 day journey, plus only 2 of over a million lived

147

to see the promised land. Complaining shows a lack of faith in God and His plan. It also opens up a door into the spiritual realm that allows hindering spirits to come in and slow or stop the flow of God's prosperity into your life.

2. **Rejoice daily in the blessings**. God has given each of us so much to be grateful for. We should be living each day with an attitude of gratitude. Rejoice each day in the blessings you have right now and those that are on the way. If you start feeling down or begin questioning God, turn on some worship music and break out the Bible and start reading His prosperity promises for you. Then rejoice some more! The Apostle Paul is such a great example. Even when he was in chains in prison he would praise God and sing songs of worship. He had learned to rejoice daily in his blessings, no matter what the physical circumstances.

3. **Build up your account**. There are so many people who go to God with their petitions for prosperity and God wants to do it, but then the devil comes along and says, "hold on a moment, let's see if this person has anything in their account." It's like walking into your bank and asking them for a million dollars. They say, "Ok, let's see how much you have in your account." If you don't have a million dollars in your account, they aren't going to give it to you. It's the same with God's prosperity system. When you asked Jesus into your heart and were saved, you opened an account with the World Bank of God. As you do certain things, your account builds up and qualifies you for blessings. We've talked about these things in earlier chapters – tithing and giving. The tithe is the first 10% of your income and any increase. According to Malachi 3:10-11, you are building up your account when you tithe. In Philippians 4:17 Paul says, "Not that I am looking for a gift, but I am looking for what may be credited to your account." The second thing to do to build up your account is to give, above the tithe. Give your money, time, and talents, to help people and further the Kingdom of God. The third thing is to invest time with God through meditating on the Word, prayer, services, classes,

and fellowship with other's who are seeking God. In Mark 10, Jesus taught the disciples that if they followed Him and operated within God's plan, that they would receive great blessings both in their life on earth as well as their eternal life in heaven. As you build up your account, you are building a strong foundation, upon which God can pour out vast prosperity.

4. **Beware of the devil's schemes**. As you begin tapping into God's prosperity plan and waiting on God, the devil is going to try to derail you with his get rich quick schemes – lottery, gambling, gifting programs, chain letters, and pyramid schemes. If the promise is big money without having to do any work, then it's a scheme and should be avoided. Proverbs 10:2 says, "Ill-gotten gain has no lasting value . . ." Even if you did hit it big in one of these schemes, the prosperity wouldn't last. Earlier you read about the young couple who won 12 million dollars in the lottery and one year later they were bankrupt and divorced. The newspapers have been full of stories about people who won large amounts of money, only to find themselves worse off than they were before they won. It is because they were not prepared for wealth. Only God knows when you are ready for wealth. So, when presented with opportunities that seem "too good to be true," ask God for discernment and invest the time to carefully investigate. You will likely find that there is no substance behind the smoke and mirrors.

Let's go back to Exodus 4:13 for our third key: ". . . and see the salvation of the Lord."

Key #3: See the Prosperity of the Lord

The Hebrew word for salvation is "yashuweh" (yeesh-oo-aw) which means welfare, deliverance, victory, and prosperity. If we substitute prosperity for salvation, we get ". . . and see the prosperity of the Lord." How prosperous is God? When He shows His prosperity to a person, what happens to their life? Solomon became the richest man in the world. Brace yourself and see the prosperity of the Lord in your life. Let's see what that might look like:

Psalm 65:11 "You crown the year with your bounty and your carts <u>overflow</u> with abundance."

Proverbs 3:9-10 "Honor the Lord with your wealth, with the firstfruits of all your crops; then your barns will be filled to <u>overflowing</u> and your vats will brim over with new wine."

Joel 2:24 "The threshing floors will be filled with grain; the vats will <u>overflow</u> with new wine and oil."

Zechariah 1:17 "Proclaim further: This is what the Lord Almighty says: 'My towns will again <u>overflow</u> with prosperity, and the Lord will again comfort Zion and choose Jerusalem.'"

Malachi 3:10 "Bring the whole tithe into the storehouse, that there may be food in my house. Test me in this, 'says the Lord Almighty, 'and see if I will not throw open the floodgates of heaven and pour out so much blessing that <u>you will not have room enough for it</u>."

Did you notice the abundance in all of these scriptures? Blessings of different types are brimming over or overflowing. Wouldn't you like God to pour out so much financial blessing that you don't have room enough for it? That's what He is preparing to do.

Ok, back to Exodus 14:13 for the final key: ". . . which He will accomplish for you today."

Key #4: God Will Accomplish It for You

As we discussed in Chapter 5, partnership with God has privileges. This part of Exodus 14:13 shows that God has a part in this, since He is going to accomplish it for you. You've already completed your part by doing all the things that were outlined in the previous chapters. When you do your part, it allows God to do His, which is to create increase. Earlier you read in 1st Corinthians 3:6, "I planted the seed, Apollos watered it, but <u>God made it grow</u>." Our part is to plant the see in good soil (ministry) and then let God make it grow.

This last portion of Exodus 14:13 clearly indicates that God is working for you right now. All you have to do is continue doing your part and then wait and see the prosperity of the Lord! Prosperity is on its way to you. No matter what your circumstances, fear not, God is bigger than they are. Enter into God's prosperity plan, then stand – position yourself and wait on God. Watch and see God's prosperity pour into your life. The scripture says He <u>will</u> accomplish it, not He might, or He could, so there is no question about Him accomplishing it for you. Just keep doing your part, be patient, and persevere through the trials. Great prosperity will be yours very soon.

Chapter Eight Discussion Questions

1. Are you doing all the things that you learned in the first seven chapters? Discuss.

2. What fears are you dealing with as you wait for God's prosperity? Discuss.

3. Who are the dream stealers in your life? Discuss how you could better handle them.

4. Discuss your current financial circumstances? How would you like them to look?

5. Why is patience important at this stage of God's plan? Discuss.

6. Are you experiencing God's joy in your circumstances? Discuss.

7. Do you find yourself complaining about your circumstances? Discuss.

8. What are you doing to build up your God account? Discuss.

9. Have you been approached with any schemes? Discuss.

10. Do you truly believe that God is going to pour abundant prosperity into your life?

11. What is your part in God's plan? What is God's part? Discuss.

Nine

Practical Keys
To Prosperity

Chapter 9

Practical Keys to Prosperity

The devil has done an excellent job of deceiving Americans into thinking they need all the material things and that they should use credit to buy these things. Statistically, the average American has $7,000 in credit card debt. Most people we know have much more than that. Credit card debt in the U.S. is at epidemic proportions! Romans 13:8 says, "Keep out of debt and owe no man anything . . ." Debt has been one of the tools that the devil has used to bind God's children and keep them from living life to the fullest. The problem with debt is that we often have to check our financial situation before we can give or help. There are many things that God might want us to do, but we can't because of debt.

God also doesn't like debt, because it makes His children servants to their lenders. Proverbs 22:7 says, "The rich rule over the poor, and the borrower is servant to the lender." God is jealous of who we serve. Matthew 6:24 reads, "No one can serve two masters. Either he will hate the one and love the other, or he will be devoted to the one and despise the other. You cannot serve both God and money." If you are in debt, you are serving money and God doesn't want you serving money. When you have to focus on the debt every day, it takes your focus away from Kingdom work. Debt is a consequence of the world's prosperity plan and not a part of God's prosperity plan. Also, when you are in debt, much of the money that God has given you is going out in interest, instead of being used to expand the Kingdom.

God did not intend His children to be in debt. Instead, He wants us to lend to nations. Deuteronomy 28:12-13 reads, "The Lord will open the heavens, the storehouse of his bounty, to send rain on your land in season and to bless all the work of your hands. You will lend to many nations; but will borrow from none. The Lord will make you the head, not the tail. If you pay attention to the commands of the Lord your God that I give you this day and carefully follow them, you will always be at the top, never at the bottom." This scripture promises that God will pour out His blessing upon you, so that you can literally lend to nations and not have to borrow from anyone. When you are a lender, you are the head; whereas when you are a borrower, you are the tail. It's time to get our tail in gear and get out of debt!

God intended for His children to be prosperous in every way. Unfortunately, many people have not been patient with God's plan and have tried to take control by borrowing money in order to enter into the world's prosperity plan. The world's plan has put people into financial bondage through mortgages, car loans, lines of credit, home equity loans, and credit cards. In God's plan, we will pay cash for everything. This is probably hard to believe, but God's wealth is endless and according to His promises, He wants to open up the windows of heaven and pour out His prosperity on those who position themselves to receive the flow of His plan. When He does this, there will be so much wealth that you will have trouble keeping track of it all. Imagine if God put you in a position where He was providing you with an income of $100,000 a month (we know a number of Christians who are earning at this level or greater). You could save a few months and purchase your dream home. Then you could live on 20% or $20,000 a month and give away $80,000 each month to help people in need and further the work of the Kingdom. This is an example that may be unimaginable to you, but is probably miniscule to God. Based on what He did for Solomon and David, $100,000 per month would be a pittance! How about if we allow God's plan to work to its fullest?

In the rest of this chapter, you will learn some practical ways to eliminate current debt and to stay out of debt. Many of these ideas have come from the book <u>The Debt Terminator</u> by John Avanzini. This is a great little book, by a Christian author, that is packed with powerful information that can help you get out of debt. If you take this information to heart, within a relatively short period of time, you could be completely out of debt and can then use that extra money to help further the Kingdom.

Debt Reduction Plan

Most people are so totally overwhelmed by their debt that they cannot imagine a way out. Some are even considering bankruptcy, which again is part of the world's plan, but not part of God's plan. Here is a program that many people have used to get themselves out from under a mountain of debt. The first step is to make a list of all your debt – mortgage, credit cards, lines of credit, car loans, etc. Include in your list the name of the creditor, amount owed, monthly payment, interest rate, and due date.

The second step is to total the monthly payment column, so that you have one lump sum. This is your minimum monthly payment and will remain so until you are completely out of debt.

The third step is to select the lowest balance account and do whatever you need to do in order to pay extra on that account. If possible, double the payment, but at very least pay the interest amount on top of the actual payment. If there is no extra money right now, think of creative ways you could make some extra money – garage or yard sale, home business, part-time job, craft sale, etc. Pay that account off as quickly as possible.

The fourth step begins once you have paid off that first account. Identify the next lowest balance account and begin adding the amount you were paying on the account you just paid off. Continue paying off accounts, identifying the next lowest balance, and adding to the payment, until all of your debt is eliminated. Be patient, as it will be slow at first, but as you get a couple accounts paid off, you will pick up momentum. Once you have paid off all of your credit accounts, it's time to move on to the mortgage.

Karen and I (Rod) have had a mountain of debt for years. What is a mountain? Well at one point, due to bad business dealings, times of unemployment, and not operating in God's plan, we had $120,000 in debt (not including our mortgage). To us this amount of debt seemed like a literal mountain and was an incredible burden on our marriage and family. The majority of our decisions had to be focused on money issues and financial survival. It also inhibited us from fully operating in God's plan.

A few years ago we started on the debt reduction program described above and, because of our faithfulness; God has blessed us with increased income, which has allowed us to pay things off quicker. That mountain now looks like a small hill. With God's continued blessings and strength to continue our disciplined plan, our debt will be completely paid off this year. We found two keys: The first is to have a written plan that is birthed out of prayer. Go to God and ask for His plan to remove the debt and then do what He says. He asked us to sell our home and one of our cars. He also asked us to downsize our home twice, as our children moved out. As you listen to God, He will ask you to do some things that aren't comfortable, but if you do them, He will reward you.

The second key was to ask God for opportunities to make some extra money, which could be used to pay off larger chunks of debt. We did this and He provided many opportunities in the form of part-time jobs, garage or yard sales, selling stuff on E-Bay, and a part-time business. It would have been real easy to use this extra money for fun things such as vacations, clothes, or entertainment, but we had committed to God to pay off debt and so we did. So, if you have a mountain of debt, ask God for some opportunities to earn extra income and then use that income to quickly reduce the debt.

Rapid Mortgage Elimination

Mortgage companies and banks very rarely even talk about anything but a 30-year loan, primarily because it's their best way of making money. Have you ever studied the amount of interest you are paying on a 30-year mortgage? The interest typically doubles the total amount you pay for a house. In this section, you will learn a number of techniques for reducing the interest you pay on a mortgage. You'll have to check with your mortgage lender to see if they allow these strategies or select one that does.

First Day Payment Strategy – Most people provide a down payment check upon closing a home and initiating a mortgage. The first payment isn't due until 30 days later. This results in 30 days of interest on the full amount of the mortgage. If you have the funds, pay one or more payments before the first payment is due. The earlier you pay them, the greater the savings – day one would be the best. Here is an example of the savings (from The Debt Terminator by John Avanzini) if your loan amount is $100,000, the term is 30 years, and the interest is 8%. Your payment would be $733.76 per month and if you made just one extra payment on day one, it would save you $7,308.23 and shave 11 months off the loan. If you made 3 payments in advance, you would save $19,792.74 and eliminate 30 months. By making 5 payments ($3,668.80) on day one of the loan, you would reduce the loan by $30,797.67 and cut the loan length to just 26 years and one month. Although, not as effective, this will work with existing mortgages, just make the extra payments any time and it will reduce the principle, which reduces the total interest you will pay and the amount of time necessary to pay off the loan.

Split Payment Strategy – Mortgages are always set-up so that you make one payment a month. This is excellent for the financial institution, as they get a full month's worth of interest on the entire balance. Another excellent strategy for reducing interest and the length of the loan is to make a half payment every two weeks, instead of once a month. Because you are making 26 half payments, you will make one extra payment a year. There are two benefits of using this strategy. The first is that each time you make a payment you are reducing your principle, thus reducing the interest paid. Second, you make one extra payment a year, which accomplishes the same thing. Let's see what the affect would be on that same loan scenario we used earlier. Instead of making payments of $733.76 per month, you would make payments of $366.88 every two weeks. On a $100,000 loan at 8% interest, you would save $49,298.43 in interest and reduce the loan by 7 years and 2 months (this example is also from The Debt Terminator by John Avanzini).

Increased Payment Strategy – Just because the mortgage company establishes your monthly payment doesn't mean that's what you have to pay. Any amount you add on to your payment goes straight to principle and reduces the total amount of interest and the term of the loan. This strategy works with both new and existing loans.

Shorter Term Strategy – As was mentioned earlier, mortgage companies and banks will always offer a 30-year loan, as they make the most on that loan. However, there are other lengths of loans available if you just ask. Typically a 15-year mortgage payment will be only a couple hundred dollars more a month than a 30-year loan and you are paying 15 less years. For example, that $100,000 loan at 8% interest would have a payment of $733.76 over 30 years or $955.65 over 15 years. If you went the 15-year route, you'd save yourself $92,136.60!

Lower Interest Strategy – Financial institutions are always offering re-financing and home equity loans. If you can lower your interest rate by even 1%, do it, as it will save you a bunch of money over the term of the loan. However, avoid the temptation to pay the lower payment. Instead, continue paying your old, higher payment. The difference between old and new payments will go towards principle and reduce both interest paid and term.

Credit Card Strategies

In the beginning God made man and woman naked, so they wouldn't have any pockets for credit cards. Maybe not, but we do know that God does not like interest. Leviticus 25:36 says, "Do not take interest of any kind from him . . ." Deuteronomy 23:19 reads, "Do not charge your brother interest, whether on money or food or anything else that may earn interest." We must then assume that God does not like credit cards. However, they are a huge part of the world's prosperity plan and many people are deeply in credit card debt. In this section, you will learn some strategies for eliminating credit card debt.

Debit Card Strategy – If you don't already have a Visa/MasterCard debit card, talk with your bank and order one. It has the same power as a credit card – secure hotel rooms and rental cars by phone, order merchandise over the phone or on the Internet, and use for automatic payments. The key is that instead of incurring debt when you make a purchase, the money comes directly out of your bank account. That way you can never build up debt over time by making purchases with the thought that you'll pay off the credit card right away. Interest, on a credit card, is being charged every day you don't make that payment and it runs up the total quickly. Since there is never an interest charge when using your debit card, you will never have this problem. Cut up all your credit cards and use only your debit card from this point on.

Lower Interest Strategy – Make a list of all your credit cards with the interest rate, balance, and monthly payment. Search for cards that offer a much lower interest rate and do some consolidating. If the reduction in interest or the consolidation of several cards into one reduces the payment, continue paying the larger amount you are now paying, so you can pay it off quicker. Make sure you read all the fine print on those low interest offers. Some offer a very low percentage for a limited period of time and then the interest rate skyrockets after the promotion period. Many also charge high transaction fees for transferring balances from other cards and an annual renewal fee. If you are going to transfer balances over from a higher interest card to one that has a lower interest rate, find one that has no transaction or annual fees and either a low fixed rate right from the beginning or a card with a low rate for a period of time and then a fixed rate that is lower than your current rate.

Consolidation Strategy – Many financial institutions offer home equity loans or lines of credit. If you can find one with a lower rate than you are paying on your credit cards, consolidate all of them into one loan. Again, if this reduces the total payment, continue paying the higher payment and pay the loan off quicker. If this loan is attached to your home, the interest is tax deductible. However, do not roll credit card bills or auto loans into a home re-financing or you may end up paying those loans over 30 years and increase your total interest payments.

Accelerated Payment Strategy – Much like a mortgage, credit card companies only require you to make one payment a month. Most people make the minimum payment. This keeps them indebted for long periods of time, sometimes years, as so little of the payment actually goes toward the principle. If you would like to get rid of the credit cards quicker, make a payment every time you get paid. This will accelerate your payoff and reduce your debt quickly.

If you are serious about getting totally out of debt, get a Visa/MasterCard debit card and cut up all your credit cards, then use the strategies you just learned to eliminate the credit card debt once and for all.

Auto Loan Strategies

Although an auto loan is secured by the vehicle, automobiles depreciate in value and quite often are worth less than what you owe after just a year of payments. Many of the same principles that we discussed in regards to credit cards and mortgages, apply here also. Financial institutions make money by charging you interest when you finance a car, so the first rule of thumb is to shop for financing. Don't just accept the financing the dealer offers. Check with your bank, other banks, and particularly with credit unions, as they typically offer better rates on car loans. Find the best rate possible and then go through the process of being pre-qualified for an auto loan. Make sure that there aren't any pre-payment penalties, as our goal will be to pay the car off much quicker than the loan term. Once you are pre-qualified, you know exactly the amount to have to spend and can walk into a dealer and make a cash offer. This will give you much greater negotiating power and will keep you from buying more car than you need.

If you have a trade-in, sell it yourself. You will always get more for it by selling it, than by trading in at a dealership. Check your city to see if they have any of the publications that have cars for sale by private owners. You'll find them in racks at the grocery store. Call the publisher and find out what it costs to sell your car through the publication. Usually it's not very expensive and cars that are priced fairly often sell quickly. Check the publication and your local newspaper for other cars like yours to determine a range of pricing. You can also review the Blue Book value by visiting the following web site http://www.kbb.com. On that site you will find many great tips for selling your car and buying a new one.

Most people try to pay as little down on a car as possible, when actually you should pay as much down as you can. So, sell your car first and then apply what you make on that sale as a down payment. Add as much available cash as you can, so that the principle amount is as low as possible. This will reduce your total interest payments.

As with credit cards and your mortgage, you can increase the amount of your payment or make double payments. Whenever you get a financial windfall, pay large chunks toward your auto loan. Set a goal to pay off your auto loan in a maximum of 30 months. You will likely keep that car for at least five years, so even after you have paid off the loan, continue making the payments into a bank account and by the time you are ready to buy a new car, you will have enough to pay cash. Then you can continue making the payments into your bank account and build up quite a nest egg. Let's see how that might work. Let's say that you were paying $500 per month toward the car loan and paid it off in 30 months. You keep the car an additional 30 months, making that $500 payment into a bank account. At the end of the 60 months, you own the car free and clear and have amassed $15,000 plus interest in an account. Sell your car and purchase a car for the amount you have available. If you continued making your $500 payment into the bank account and kept the new car for five years, you would have $30,000 plus interest and the value of your car to purchase your next car. Just keep repeating the process and you will always be able to pay cash for your cars.

Debt Termination

If you are serious about getting totally out of debt, you will need a plan. On the following pages you will find a worksheet that you can use to create a master debt termination plan and to track your progress. Use these forms to get started right away. God has big plans for you. Remember that Jeremiah 29:11 says, "For I know the plans I have for you," declares the Lord, "plans to prosper you and not to harm you, plans to give you hope and a future." God wants to make you prosperous, but He needs you out of debt first. Make a plan; work the plan, and position yourself for abundance!

Debt Termination Worksheet

Income:

Total monthly net income (what you actually receive)	$
Additional income you could earn	$
Total Monthly Income Available	$

Expenses:

Total fixed expenses (mortgage/rent, utilities, food, etc)	$
Total credit card payments	$
Total other loan payments (excluding mortgage and auto)	$
Total automobile payments	$
Total Monthly Expenses	$

Debt Reduction:

Fixed expenses reduction plan –

Credit card payment reduction plan –

Loan payment reduction plan –

Automobile payment reduction plan –

Notes:

Chapter Nine Discussion Questions

1. How much credit card/loan debt do you have? Discuss how you got there.

2. Why doesn't God like interest? Discuss.

3. What would your life be like if you were earning $100,000 a month?

4. Make a list of your credit cards and make up a plan to pay them off.

5. What opportunities do you have to make some extra money? Discuss.

6. Which mortgage reduction strategy would work best for your situation? Discuss.

7. What is the difference between a credit and debit card? Discuss.

8. Discuss your car situation and determine if there are some ways to reduce costs.

9. What does God say about His plan for you in Jeremiah 29:11? Discuss.

10. Use the Debt Elimination worksheet to begin the process.

Ten

Uncovering Your Personal Prosperity Plan

Chapter 10

Uncovering Your Prosperity Plan

In this chapter, you will uncover your own prosperity plan, based on what you've learned in the rest of the book. The first order of business will be to get your house in order. What if God were coming to visit your home, you would invest some time to clean it up, wouldn't you? Well, he wants to visit your financial house right now, so it's time to get it cleaned up. Next you will work on your dreams and goals. If you are like most people, the world has beaten you down over the years and you don't have many dreams or goals left. God loves it when we dream and set goals, so you will learn how to discover your dreams all over again or perhaps for the very first time. After that will be a reminder of the prosperity promises that God has made and how you can apply them to your daily life. Finally you will complete a prosperity agreement. God has been making covenants with man since the beginning of mans existence. This is your chance to make a prosperity covenant with God.

Getting Your House in Order

Step One: Analyze

The first step is to analyze your current financial situation. Here, you will make a list of your assets (those things you own that have value - house, car, property, rentals, jewelry, vehicles, furniture, investments, coins, 401K or other retirement funds, cash value in life insurance, savings bonds, etc. If you are married, work with your spouse to develop this list. Invest the time necessary to get everything on the list.

Step Two: What to Keep

The second step is to determine what you want to keep. Most people keep a lot of things that they don't need anymore and by selling these things, they could create another source of income that could be used to pay off debt or invest into Kingdom work. Evaluate each item and ask God if you should keep it or sell it. Remember that although these things have some value in our world, they have no eternal value. Jesus taught us not to store up treasures on earth, but rather to store up treasures in heaven (Matthew 6:19). When you pass on from this life, you will not take any of those material things with you, but you will be judged by the treasures you laid up in heaven – in other words what you did with your money, time, and talents that furthered the Kingdom of God here on earth.

Step Three: What to Sell

The third step is to determine which of these items you will sell and make up a plan to sell them. You could have a garage or yard sale, advertise in the paper, or contact a broker or antique dealer, or set up a selling account on E-bay to begin the process of selling these items. Use the money you earn to either pay off debt or plant it into ministries that are doing Kingdom work.

Step Four: What to Give

The fourth step is to determine what items you will give away. Perhaps you have people in your life that could really use what you have.   You could also donate vehicles, property, houses, jewelry, coins, investments, etc. to your church, as they could sell them and use the money to build the Kingdom of God. Also, these would be tax deductions for you. Ask God to reveal what items He wants you to give.

Step Five: Debt

The fifth step is to analyze your debt or what you owe. Make a list of all your debts – mortgage, auto loans, credit cards, etc.   Using the strategies you learned in the last chapter, write a plan for how you will eliminate all the debt. Write out a plan to eliminate your credit card debt by starting with the lowest balance account and continuing to add the payments to new accounts as you pay off accounts. Include an accelerated mortgage and auto loan payoff plan. You can use the debt elimination plan you formulated in the last chapter to help you with this step.

Step Six: Savings

The sixth step is to analyze your current savings and make a plan to build up an emergency fund. Make sure you have paid off all your credit card debt before beginning a savings program, as you will not likely earn an interest rate higher than you are paying on the cards. Once you have paid off all your credit card debt, begin building your emergency fund. This will take care of you in the case of car troubles, medical or dental emergencies, etc. You don't need to have a lot of extra money sitting around in bank accounts, but enough to where you won't get blindsided by the enemy.

Step Seven: Expenses

The seventh step is to develop a plan for reducing your expenses. First, identify all your expenses (other than debt) – utilities, cable TV, newspaper, magazine subscriptions, club memberships, food, gasoline, etc. Analyze whether there are any of those that could be eliminated or reduced. Although these things may be enjoyable in this life, remember that they have no eternal value, so be honest about what you really need and eliminate the rest. Wherever possible, hunt for better rates in order to save money that can be used for Kingdom business or to pay off debt.

Step Eight: Budget

The eighth step is to develop a monthly budget. 10% of gross (before taxes) income would go toward your tithe and 10% toward giving, and the other 80% is yours for living. However, if you are in a position to live on 70%, then include 10% for savings or investments. Your long-range goal should be to reverse those numbers; living on 20% and tithing 10% and giving 70%. Imagine what the world would be like if every person gave 70% of their monthly income to help those in need. That's the vision God has for our world.

Step Nine: Blockades

The ninth step is to analyze the current and potential blockades to achieving your goals. Evaluate the physical blockades – current limitations to your income, physical disabilities that inhibit your income, etc. Next, look at the mental or psychological blockades – what are you thinking that would limit your income potential, what past mental programming is inhibiting your income potential, etc. Then determine if you have any spiritual barriers. Do you fully believe that God loves you and wants you to prosper? If not, then every day you need to review the prosperity scriptures that you'll find at the end of the book. Lastly, develop a plan for eliminating all these blockades. If you are struggling with how to eliminate your particular blockades, ask God and also seek godly counsel – a Pastor, deacon, elder, or a godly person who is mature in their walk with God. Do not move forward until you have a clear plan for eliminating your blockades.

To facilitate the development and implementation of this plan, use the Master Plan form in Appendix A. Your plan must be in writing in order for it to be effective and you'll need to update it regularly, as your circumstances change. Celebrate your victories, but don't condemn yourself if things don't go quite as planned. Remember that you have a very real spiritual enemy who is seeking to destroy your life.

There will be setbacks, but with God all things are possible and if you stay within His plan, ultimately you will win the battle.

Dreams and Goals

Dreamers built our world. If there were no people with big dreams, there would be no great inventions. Unfortunately, our schools and the system itself do not encourage dreaming. Many people were dreamers in their younger days, but those dreams have been squelched by the overwhelming reality of family, responsibilities, work, and financial struggles. God is a dreamer and we are made in His image. He dreamed of a perfect world with beings who could love Him and He created the earth and then Adam and Eve. When mankind sinned, He dreamed of reconciling mankind to Him by sending His Son Jesus to earth to die on a cross as an atoning sacrifice for the past, present, and future sins of all mankind. He dreamed of a day when there would be no evil in the earth and He could bring His heavenly realm back to earth and once again commune with His creation. According to the book of Revelation, this will happen, so all of us who are born again can look forward to that day! The most exciting thing is that God dreamed all these things while He hovered over the void that is now our universe and He has seen all His dreams come true.

Your next step in creating a Master Plan is to do some dreaming. You'll need a pad, pen, and some kind of timer you can set for five minutes that will give you a verbal alarm. During that five-minute period you will be writing everything you would like to do, buy, and be. You'll also want to write down anyone you'd like to meet and all the places you like to go. There are no financial or time limitations. You now have an unlimited income and total time freedom, so let your mind run wild. Don't let inhibitions or so-called realities get in the way of your dreaming. Remember that all things are possible with God and that you are at the beginning stages of tapping into His limitless financial plan. Ok, set your timer and start writing. When you are done, include these on your Master Plan form. STOP READING.

Well how did you do? Did you find that the ideas flowed easily or did you struggle? Did you question whether you could really do or have those things that came to mind? Well, God created your mind to dream and anything that comes into your mind is possible. It's the enemy who is trying to limit you, so don't let him.

Next, you're going to describe your dream home. Where will it be located? How big will it be? What will the rooms look like? How about the yard/property? Will you have a pool? What's the view like? Again, there are no limitations, God wants you prosperous and enjoying life. He just wants you focused on Him and not on the money and the things money will buy. So keep your eyes on God and He will provide your heart's desire. Take a few minutes to describe in minute detail your dream home on the Master Plan form. STOP READING.

Ok, now that you know what your dream home will look like, how about your dream car. Most people drive what they can afford. Some people use credit to drive more than what they can afford. Someone once said that everyone could afford a Rolls Royce; they just might have to live in it. What is your dream car? What color? What amenities? What's the interior like? God provided Solomon with many dream cars, so again, if you are focused on God, He will make your dreams come true. Take the time right now to describe your dream car on the Master Plan form. STOP READING.

Lastly, would be your dream vacations. Most people can't afford really nice vacations. But with God all things are possible. Set your imagination free to dream up incredible vacations. Remember that there are no limitations. You have all the money you will ever need and all the time in the world, so you can go wherever you want and stay for however long you want. Describe your dream vacations on the Master Plan form. STOP READING.

God knows your every thought, but just like a good father likes to hear the dreams of his kids, God wants to hear about your dreams. Put your dream home, car, and vacations into a prayer and pray it every day. God wants to know your heart's desire, so that in His timing He can fulfill them. Write these prayers on your Master Plan form now. STOP READING.

If you are married, make sure that you include your spouse in the development of the Master Plan. Include children who are old enough to understand as well. If your entire family is involved in the development of the plan, they will all have ownership and you will be in unity.

Goals

Dreams are great, but God wants you to be involved in the process. He wants to help you develop goals, based on your dreams and a plan to achieve those goals. We know that God is a goal setter, because in Luke 13:32, Jesus says, "He replied, 'Go tell that fox, I will drive out demons and heal people today and tomorrow, and on the third day I will reach my goal." His goal, of course was death on a cross, a quick trip to hell to defeat death and lead the captives out, and then to be resurrected into a new life. If Jesus had a goal when He was born into this world, don't you think that God birthed you with goals as well?

Our first and primary goal is outlined in Matthew 28:19, where Jesus tells us, "Therefore go and make disciples of all nations, baptizing them in the name of the Father and of the Son and of the Holy Spirit." We are to plant the Word of God into our heart and share it with others who don't know the Lord. What are you doing to accomplish this goal on a regular basis? Include your description of this goal and your action plan for accomplishing the goal, in the Master Plan form. STOP READING.

Second, God has a personal goal for each individual. You are completely unique in this and God has given you something completely unique to do. He has also given you specific gifts, skills, talents, abilities, knowledge, and experiences that will help you achieve this goal. You may already have a good idea what that goal is, but if not, ask God to reveal it to you. Be patient, as He may not reveal it immediately or He may reveal it in pieces. Once you understand your goal, ask God daily to help you establish smaller goals to achieve that life goal. Include this goal in your Master Plan form. STOP READING.

Third, God wants you to live a prosperous life and earlier, He helped you to create your dream house, car, and vacation. Now it's time to ask Him to help you set goals to achieve those dreams. Keep in mind that even though your current circumstances may make it seem impossible to achieve these dreams, all things are possible with God. The key to the life of your dreams is faith; faith that if you give it all up to God, He will provide all your needs and many of your wants. Complete these sections in your Master Plan form now. STOP READING.

For many years I (Rod) had a dream of publishing a book. In 1987 I wrote my first manuscript, which to date has never been published. However, I never let that dream die and continued to set goals. Eight years later God arranged for my first published book (Successful Network Marketing for the 21st Century, Oasis Press). Then God used that as a vehicle to create a financial base, which allows me to be a full-time writer and speaker. God will give you dreams and goals that may seem impossible. It also may take many years for you to see those dreams come true, but never let them die. Continue to set goals and believe that God-given dreams will come true.

It is quite possible that the devil has put you into a box financially. In other words you have financial limitations based on the job you have. It's a classic case of not being able to see the forest for the trees. You're in the middle of it all and can't see outside the box. However, God has a view of the big picture, so why not ask Him to guide you out of the box and onto the path He has for you. He may want you to go back to school to learn new skills that would increase your income or He may provide you with an investment opportunity or a home business idea. Be open to whatever He gives you. Don't be like the man of God who fully trusted in the Lord and when it was reported that his town was going to be flooded; he said that the Lord would keep him safe. Emergency workers came by to tell him that he should evacuate, but he just replied that the Lord would keep him safe. As the water rose up to the second story window, a boat came along to take him to safety, but he just replied that the Lord would keep him safe. As the water reached the roof-line, a helicopter swooped in to take him to safety, but he refused to go, replying that the Lord would keep him safe. The water covered his house and swept him into the raging water and he drowned. When he arrived in heaven, he asked God why He didn't keep him safe. God replied, "give me a break, I sent an emergency worker, a boat, and a helicopter, what more did you want?" Keep your eyes open to the opportunities that God places in front of you. Sometimes they will look very ordinary, but if you are talking with God every day, you will recognize the doors He is opening for you.

Well, that's it, you now know everything necessary to fully enter into God's plan and have developed your own Master Plan. Review your plan every day and invest time with God each morning and night to make sure you are following the plan. Keep your eyes focused on God and make sure you don't get caught up in materialism and the world's plan. Deuteronomy 8:18 teaches that it is God who gives us the power to get wealth. Proverbs 10:22 tells us that the "blessing of the Lord brings wealth, and he adds no trouble to it." Finally, according to Ecclesiastes 5:19, "When God gives any man wealth and possessions, and enables him to enjoy them, accept his lot and be happy in his work – it is a gift of God." God has given you the power to create massive wealth and He wants you to accept it as a gift from your loving Heavenly Father. Seek Him in prayer and position yourself to receive His gift of prosperity; He's waiting for you with the anticipation of a loving Father.

Appendix A
Master Plan Worksheet

Get Your House In Order:

1. **Assets** – make a list of everything you own that has value. This would include your home, rental properties, property, vehicles, furniture, investments, savings, coins, retirement plans, cash value in life insurance, etc. List them below, along with their estimated value.

Now, determine what assets you will keep, sell, and give away:

Keep –

Sell –

Give Away –

2. **Debt** – here you will list what you owe. Include the name of the debtor, the total amount, monthly payment, interest rate, and payment date.

Credit Cards –

Mortgage –

Loans –

3. **Debt Reduction Plan** – in this section you will describe how you will eliminate your debt over time. Refer back to the strategies in order to create your plan.

Credit Card Payoff –

Mortgage –

Loans –

3. **Blockades** – in this section you will describe the actual and potential blockades that could keep you from accomplishing your goal of complete debt elimination.

Physical –

Mental –

Spiritual –

Plan to eliminate or avoid blockades –

Dreams and Goals:

Dreams – here is where you list the dreams from your 5 minutes of dreaming.

Dream Career – describe your perfect career.

Dream Home – here is where you describe in detail, your dream home.

Dream Car – here is where you describe in detail, your dream car.

Dream Vacation – here is where you describe your dream vacation.

Prayers for dream career, home, car, and vacation –

Goals:

We all have the goal of spreading the good news about Jesus Christ and making disciples. In the following space list the steps you are taking to accomplish this goal.

God has also given you a personal goal. Describe what you know of this goal in the following space.

God gives us great dreams and then will aid us in developing goals, which are the steps necessary in order to achieve our dreams. In the following section, you will write the goals that are necessary to achieve the dreams mentioned in the last section.

Goals for Dream Career – what steps are necessary in order for you to start enjoying your dream career (i.e. research, training, interviewing, etc.)?

Goals for Dream House – what steps are necessary in order for you to live in your dream home (i.e. research, searching, blueprints, financial plan, etc.)?

Goals for Dream Car – what steps are necessary in order for you to have your dream car (i.e. research, showroom visit, financial plan, etc.)?

Goals for Dream Vacation – what steps are necessary in order for you to go on your dream vacation (i.e. research, travel agent, internet, financial plan, time plan, etc.)?

Seed Plan:

As you learned earlier in the book, you will not reap a financial harvest (and achieve your dreams) unless you plant seeds. In the spaces below invest the time to develop a seed plan.

Tithe (10% of your gross income and increase) – if you are already tithing, then begin standing on the promises in Malachi 3:10-12. If you are not tithing or not tithing correctly, then write a promise to God in this space.

Giving (anything above the tithe) – write a giving plan in this space. Include the ministries you will give to, the monthly amounts, and the total percentage of your income. Also include a plan to increase your giving by a percentage or fixed amount each month or quarter.

Alms – set aside a certain amount of money each week that you give to people in need that you encounter in your every day life or that you seek out. Write a plan in this space which includes the weekly amount and the methods of distribution.

Now that you have completed your Master Plan, review and pray over it every day. Ask God to guide you to do the things that will lead to the fulfillment of your plan. Remember that the Plan will be completed in God's timing, not yours, so be patient with the process and you will reap tremendous rewards.

Appendix B

Prosperity Scriptures / Promises from God

Genesis 26:12-14 "Then Isaac sowed seed in the land and received in the same year a hundred times as much as he had planted . . ."

Deuteronomy 8:18 "But you shall remember the Lord your God, for it is He Who gives you power to get wealth, that He may establish His covenant which He swore to your fathers, as it is this day."

Deuteronomy 28:11 "And the Lord shall make you have a surplus of prosperity."

Deuteronomy 28:12 "The Lord shall open to you His good treasury."

Deuteronomy 29:9 "Therefore keep the words of this covenant, and do them that you may prosper in all you do."

Deuteronomy 30:9 "And the Lord your God will make you abundantly prosperous. . ."

Joshua 1:7 "Only be strong and very courageous, that you may observe to do according to all the law which Moses My servant commanded you; do not turn from it to the right hand or to the left, that you may prosper wherever you go."

Joshua 1:8 "This book of the law shall not depart from your mouth, but you shall meditate in it day and night, that you may observe to do according to all that is written in it. For then you will make your way prosperous, and then you will have good success."

1 Kings 2:3 "And keep the charge of the LORD your God: to walk in His ways, to keep His statutes, His commandments, His judgments, and His testimonies, as it is written in the Law of Moses, that you may prosper in all that you do and wherever you turn."

1 Chronicles 22:13 "Then you will prosper, if you take care to fulfill the statutes and judgments with which the LORD charged Moses concerning Israel. Be strong and of good courage; do not fear nor be dismayed."

2 Chronicles 26:5 "He set himself to seek God in the days of Zechariah, who instructed him in the things of God; and as long as he sought the Lord, God made him prosper."

Job 21:13 "They spend their days in prosperity…"

Job 36:10-11 "He also opens their ear to instruction, And commands that they turn from iniquity. If they obey and serve Him, They shall spend their days in prosperity, And their years in pleasures."

Psalm 1:1-3 "Blessed is the man who does not walk in the counsel of the wicked or stand in the way of sinners or sit in the seat of mockers. But his delight is in the law of the Lord, and on His law, he meditates day and night. He is like a tree planted by a stream of water, which yields its fruit in season and whose leaf does not wither. Whatever he does prospers."

Psalm 23:11 "The Lord is my Shepard; I shall not want."

Psalm 34:10 "The lions may grow weak and hungry, but those who seek the LORD lack no good thing."

Psalm 35:27 ". . . Let the Lord be magnified, who has pleasure in the prosperity of His servant."

Psalm 37:3 "Trust in the Lord instead. Be kind and good to others; then you will live safely here in the land and prosper..."

Psalm 49:16 "Do not be afraid when one becomes rich, when the glory of his house is increased."

Psalm 112:1-3 "Blessed is the man who fears the LORD, who finds great delight in his commands. His children will be mighty in the land; the generation of the upright will be blessed. Wealth and riches are in his house, and his righteousness endures forever."

Proverbs 3:9-10 "Honor the Lord with your possessions, and with the first fruits of all your increase; so your barns will be filled with plenty, and your vats will overflow with new wine."

Proverbs 10:22 "The blessing of the Lord brings wealth and He adds no trouble to it."

Proverbs 11:25 "The generous man will be prosperous . . ."

Proverbs 13:21 ". . . but prosperity is the reward of the righteous."

Proverbs 13:22 "...but the wealth of the sinner is stored up for the righteous."

Proverbs 22:7 "The rich rules over the poor and the borrower is servant to the lender."

Proverbs 28:25 "...but he who trusts in the Lord will prosper."

Ecclesiastes 5:19 "Moreover, when God gives any man wealth and possessions, and enables him to enjoy them, accept his lot and be happy in his work – this is a gift of God."

Ecclesiastes 6:2 "God gives a man wealth, possessions and honor, so that he lacks nothing his heart desires."

Isaiah 48:15 "I, even I, have spoken; yea, I have called him; I have brought him, and he shall make his way prosperous..."

Isaiah 52:13 "Behold, my servant shall deal wisely and shall prosper..."

Jeremiah 29:11 "For I know the plans I have for you, declares the Lord, plans to prosper you and not to harm you, plans to give you hope and a future."

Malachi 3:10 "'Bring the whole tithe into the storehouse, that there may be food in my house. Test me in this,' says the LORD Almighty, 'and see if I will not throw open the floodgates of heaven and pour out so much blessing that you will not have room enough for it.'"

Matthew 6:33 "But seek first the kingdom of God and His righteousness, and all these things shall be added to you."

Mark 10:29-30 "I tell you the truth," Jesus replied, "no one who has left home or brothers or sisters or mother or father or children or fields for me and the gospel will fail to receive a hundred times as much in this present age (homes, brothers, sisters, mothers, children and fields--and with them, persecutions) and in the age to come, eternal life."

Luke 6:38 "Give and it will be given to you; good measure, pressed down, shaken together, and running over will be put into your bosom. For with the same measure that you use, it will be measured back to you."

John 10:10 "I have come that they may have life, and that they may have it more abundantly."

2 Corinthians 9:6 "Remember this, whoever sows sparingly will also reap sparingly, and whoever sows generously will also reap generously."

2 Corinthians 9:10 "Now he who supplies seed to the sower and bread for food will also supply and increase your store of seed and will enlarge the harvest of your righteousness. You will be made rich in every way so that you can be generous on every occasion, and through us your generosity will result in thanksgiving to God."

Philippians 4:19 "And my God will meet all your needs according to his glorious riches in Christ Jesus."

3 John 1:2 "Beloved, I pray that you may prosper in all things and be in health, just as your soul prospers."

For information about **God's Prosperity Plan** seminars
or to order additional copies of the book,
send an email to
Rod@RodNichols.com

Appendix C
Prosperity Agreement

Father God, I confess that Your Word is the truth in my life. I agree to read Your prosperity promises every day and to speak prosperity into my everyday life. I recognize that satan has come to steal, kill, and destroy, but that Jesus came to bring life abundant and I receive that right now. I also agree to tithe 10% of my gross income and any increase, as the first check I write after being paid. I do this to show that You are truly Lord of my life. I have also developed, with Your guiding hand, a plan to reduce debt and expenses, so that I can begin giving an additional 10% or more of my gross income and increase each month as a love offering. God, I want to be a channel for your heavenly riches. As I fulfill my part, I ask that You open up the windows of heaven, so that Your abundant riches might be poured out on me. Lord I promise to plant my financial seed in fertile ground, so that You may cause an increase. I promise that as You prosper my life, it will be a testimony to You and I will stay humble and give You all the glory and honor. God, I ask Your continued wisdom, guidance, and blessing in all of my financial dealings.

_____   _____

Signature   Date